ULTRATHOUGHTS™ TRIPARTITE

INTENTIONAL THOUGHT

RECOGNIZE YOUR BIASES, LISTEN WITH AN OPEN MIND, LIVE A MORE CONTEMPLATIVE LIFE

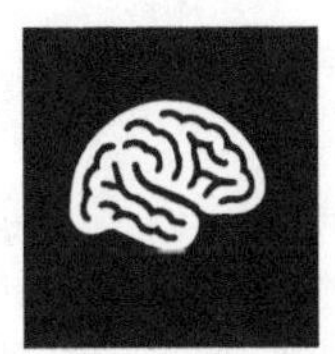

W. DURWOOD JOHNSON

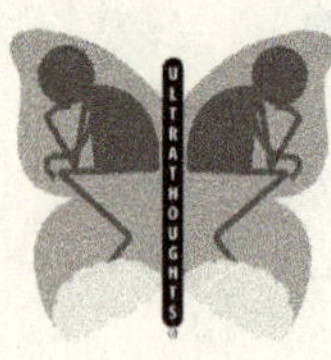

Publisher: Ultrathoughts™ LLC
ultrathoughtsbook@gmail.com
www.ultrathoughts.com

Intentional Thought: Recognize Your Bias,
Listen with an Open Mind, Live a More Contemplative Life

ISBN: 978-1-951731-00-7 (Print)
ISBN: 978-1-951731-01-4 (Ebook)
Library of Congress Control Number: 2019916539

Cover Design by Berge Design

CONTENTS

INSPIRATIONS

Special thanks to a few great musical poets.

Isaac Brock

Matt Johnson

Martin Gore

Gary Numan

David Byrne

Laurie Anderson

Richard M. Hall

Barry Andrews

PREFACE

Two sisters who happen to share little common ground indirectly form a basis for my premise. When we can recognize and suppress ideology, a fair consideration of alternative information may lead to enlightenment.

My sisters don't seem to care much about learning from each other and generally prefer not to have meaningful discussions. If they do unintentionally lurch into a discussion of substance, sparks soon fly. Though it isn't a role I seek, I eventually find myself playing peacemaker for our trio. I prefer to mediate rather than listen to their bickering. Over the years, even though I've gotten pretty good at making peace, they have gotten better at being obstinate.

Watching my sisters mature and continue to squabble, it seems to me they represent a microcosm of our society today. In the past we chose to interact with respect and compromised when necessary. We learned from each other as a result. Today it appears we are simply ignoring each other out of either simple apathy or fundamental disdain.

In fairness to my sisters—both wonderful people, I must add—I admit my inclination to do the same. I, too, often lose patience, and unfortunately respect, for those who don't think like I do. We all prefer an agreeable world, provided our own specific view is deemed superior.

This isn't anything new. Throughout the history of humanity, people have preferred to associate with those who give them affirmation, but recent technological advances are promoting the experience as never before. Without any forethought we are building a polarized society at an ever-increasing pace. Our technology is largely unregulated, and its impact is not even considered. Today we can create a type of alternative reality bubble with more depth and texture than most could imagine. The impact of this dynamic will not only change the lives of our children, it may alter our species. I challenge you to ponder the reality of the not too distant future.

Our echo chamber of truth continually feeds ideology. The coming challenges are just now starting to germinate in society as groups of people are picking sides. I don't yet understand the particulars but like many other observers I'm starting to doubt whether our leaders are prepared for what's likely to happen. Humanity seems to be reaching a crossroads. As more and more people self-select isolation within their tribe of like-minded thinkers the groups will come to resent each other.

I told you I got pretty good at peacemaking. In a way, I've revived my reluctant peacemaker role in this writing. Maybe a few more sisters will keep talking after coming to appreciate my notions.

Once we understand how and why we think as we do in the construction of our truth and reality, we will become willing to step outside our ideological self to engage our sister with respect. In doing so we will continue to learn, enhancing our truth as we foster a more cooperative society. When more members of society become willing to suppress bias in favor of respectful conversation, our world will be just a bit better than before.

INTRODUCTION

What if I told you that you would be a better person tomorrow if you reached out to someone that you generally disagree with and said; "I'll meet you at Starbucks. My treat. I want to pick your brain for a moment." Wouldn't you like to be a better person for the cost of a venti Blonde Roast Veranda Blend? Wouldn't your acquaintance be better off as well? Then why not seek that conversation?

This series of three concise books, collectively referred to as the Ultrathoughts Tripartite, will remind you that our perception is the single most important aspect of our lives. Self-created reality of mind is vastly more important than all other aspects of your life. Nothing else—not friends, work, money, family, or physical health—even comes close.

Mental narratives guide our decisions, which ultimately create our very personal version of truth. Left to our own ideological leanings, we will constantly create a biased set of truths that lead to skewed decisions. Don't misunderstand; our conclusions may be good enough, but they won't be optimal. Once we recognize the orientation of our thoughts, we can strive to resist the subtle influence of bias. By moving beyond reflexive thought we can live a more positive existence during our limited time on earth, and maybe even beyond that.

To appreciate the role perception plays in our existence is to glimpse the power of the human mind. Our mind creates the world we think we understand. Our mind's creation, the person, evolves as we mature within a society becoming a vivid representation of our ideas. These ideas, organized in more depth as we age, form an ideology or personal dogma. Some of us openly present our dogmatic self with bombast and fury; others not. However, make no mistake: we each harbor a unique ideology that frames the person we become.

Reflexive and constant acceptance of your historical ideology limits your potential. We create and internalize better ideas when we fairly consider the thoughts of others, so we should not automatically reject that which we consider outrageous. Remember that the most revolutionary ideas of mankind were deemed strange or even offensive at some point in time.

In hopes of spurring you to reconsider your own ideas, I share my views on multiple subjects throughout the series. While I have enthusiasm for my opinions and today believe every word I write, mine are not presented as a definitive truth or fact. I suggest there is no absolute truth. All is simply truth of mind. Once you internalize this statement, no enthusiasm or criticism by others will discourage you from seeking your best version of truth.

The concept of a self-determined truth is a bit foreign to our Western way of thinking. We are comforted by a "knowledge" that there is an ultimate right, wrong, black, and white. Our personal story reads easily when the rules are universal and never changing.

Regardless of our preferred assumption about truth, there are clear problems with the premise. For starters, the assumption is provably false, and, deep in our minds, we all know it. Truth is not definitive, and neither are the rules that gauge its worthiness. We willingly create the delusion we choose to live and live a life of interaction with others who do the same.

Let me give you an example of an illusionary or delusional truth. What's your favorite song? Now, ask yourself what you would have said two, ten, or twenty years ago. Was every answer the same? Of course not. The answers are relative and dependent on the story you are referencing at this moment. The truth, your truth, is not absolute. Your mind determines your truth as each second ticks by.

Today a particular song performed by the English electronic music group Above & Beyond is my favorite melody. Just thinking of it makes me happy. This is my absolute truth, my reality today. You may disagree and strongly prefer one by an American rock band, the Eagles for instance. Your statement has no bearing on my truth unless I give your belief respectful attention. Without a just consideration of your belief, there is no hope that I will change my own reality.

Ultrathoughts are better ideas, products of a mind that is fair and open, thinking from the whole brain while suppressing your historical leaning. The concept assumes we are better, society is better, when we respect each other enough to seek common ground. Certainly, it is plausible that we are all we need. However, I suggest we are best when we participate in a type of societal group therapy that seeks to recognize the special nature of any truth or reality created by our sisters and brothers. Each of us may exist isolated within our own tri-state of ideologically laced views of mind, body, and the Godhead; still, humanity is better when we interact with a mind geared toward achieving a kind of flow-state constantly open to all ideas.

Given my use of something as benign as a favorite song in an attempt to describe how ideology guides reality, you may not be convinced of my premise. After all, I did pick an ill-defined question. No scientific methodology can pick a favorite or perfect tune. Let's get more scientific.

What is the cosmic speed of light in a vacuum? Certainly, we have no disagreement regarding this question. It's settled fact; or is it? Despite what you've been indoctrinated to believe, just like the truth of a perfect melody, the question has no definitive answer for a variety of reasons—not the least of which is that many scientists can't even agree on the parameters from which to authorize a "correct" answer. The truth or reality with regards to the speed of light is not an absolute irrefutable fact. Even under ideal circumstances scientists often measure some variability.

Your personal narrative or mind-myth works hand in hand with your beliefs to create an interpretation of reality. Some of these truths are rooted in the substance of physical matter, others are not. However, we should appreciate that even a manifest truth of the physical world is no truth without validation accepted by your mind. In a fundamental sense, your relevant reality is nothing other than an interpretation: an immersive experience that is far vaster than you have been indoctrinated to believe. Reality is comprised of your mentally validated set of ideas. Reality certainly includes the material stuff of matter, atoms, but even much of that segment of reality is not relevant to you personally unless you believe it to be so.

At this very moment you have ideas, attitudes, and beliefs; vaporous concepts. All simply reside in your mind. They can be very real, yet none are physical. They are "meta" without substance. Often we neglect to appreciate the impact this kind of reality has on our lives. As ideas become embedded and organized within your personal narrative, they become the dominant factor in the continual creation of self. This immersion in a self-created illusion is what makes our species unique on the planet. Self, the person of you, can become an ideologue simply reflecting your historical narrative without any particular depth of thought. Recognizing one's willingness to consider new ideas has the potential to improve the person. It then follows that suppression of your ideology can lead to growth and possibly true enlightenment.

Your acceptance of my premise is expected, assuming the subject matter is casual or even trivial. While an Eagles fan and an Above & Beyond fan can share some laughs or even a couple of melodies, when the discussion moves to heavy subjects like child-rearing, politics, or religion, most choose not to be so fair-minded. Few of us choose to hear the opinion of a fool who disagrees with us on an important subject. What's the curse of every friendly dinner? You guessed it—somebody brought up politics or religion.

Why do we find offense in alternative points of view if deep down we know our own view is only an opinion? The simple answer is most of us aren't consciously aware of how ideology guides our interpretation of truth. We are inclined to take life as it comes and think reflexively rather than engage the mind to see past the fog of personal dogma. We are comforted when we maintain a consistent set of beliefs. Ego, your sense of self, appreciates and protects your narrative. Protective emotions are expressed in defense of your existing ideological bent. Anger and frustration offer clues that an opportunity for enlightenment may lie ahead.

Your mind functions smoothly when the rules are static, truth is not challenged, and self is never in doubt. The mind is stressed, anger results, and our story becomes jumbled when the rules keep changing or we're under attack from opposing views. For emotional comfort, we act as if rules are consistent and truth is definitive, and we ignore or disrespect challenges to our existing narrative.

Simple awareness of the role your personal story plays in your life is not enough. To manage or overcome our tendencies takes diligence, patience, and a great deal of personal humility. The mind must be driven with purposeful intent to think beyond its ideological leaning. Though most of us believe we are fair-minded and objective, without effort we are not. Most of us carry so much ideological baggage we rarely overcome its influence on our truth.

Though I may be committing reputational suicide in my efforts to explain both my premise and its beneficial application, the effort is sincere. I am no professional writer but have chosen to go without a net and share my strategy for building a more informed version of personal truth. Life is more interesting when we engage our mind with intent. The quest to build a truth without the tint of ideology is a worthy lifetime journey in search of personal enlightenment. I've noticed greater clarity, happiness, and true insight by fairly considering the views of others with whom I typically disagree. Let's have a respectful yet lively discussion that explores your truth in hopes of enlightening our own.

An important part of the premise is that from the mouths of babes come revolutionary concepts. Real thinkers are fearless; they need no one's approval or certification to contemplate any topic. Though I am neither a scientist or philosopher some of my notions may spark your own mind-bombs of brilliance that you may one day choose to put to pen. Your own memoir may not find an audience, but a sharing of your personal philosophy might just one day help the world.

Throughout the series, I touch on a number of subjects offered as a casual read. I express opinions about anthropology, the nature of science, the Godhead, religion, and even a bit of quantum mechanics as I explain my process and its benefits. No, I won't talk politics. That specific subject has gotten so repetitive it's boring.

Here in the first volume, *Intentional Thought*, I explain the challenge and introduce my idea of purposeful whole-brain thinking, a process I have termed "ultra-thinking." Key to successful ultra-thinking is a recognition that you have an ideological bent, a fundamental way of thinking. This orientation can be traced to the DNA of our species. While DNA provides a roadmap for our thoughts it is merely a suggestion and its influence can be suppressed. A second and equally important aspect of ultra-thinking is an appreciation that the only relevant truth to you is that which is validated by your contemplative mind. Mind creates your personal story or mind-myth narrative based on its evaluation of information. Nothing matters to your person unless said information is deemed relevant to mind. A truth of your mind is, in effect, your only worthy reality. Certainly, I am not suggesting there is no truth of physical fact or physical reality; however, I am proposing that, absent your belief in said truth, it has little bearing in your world. Ultra-thinking and its benefits are explained in this volume as a strategy to contest the ever-present tendency to simply follow your basic ideological leaning in hopes of creating personal Ultrathoughts.

Should you choose to join me in the next equally concise book, you will better understand the benefits of ultra-thinking. Though in theory ultra-thinking can be applied to any number of subjects in book two, *Godhead Designs,* we urge our minds to contemplate the ultimate big topic as we review history. Progressing rapidly, we review roughly a dozen Godhead ideas starting with the ancient Egyptians and ending with René Descartes. The point being to show that ideas, even ideas of the superhuman presence of God, are meta (non-substantive) products of mind. We don't disparage any view and consider these ideas as whole-brain thinkers, not arbiters of the perfect truth. Naturally, to ultra-think the Godhead one must subscribe to both suppositions as key to the process. We must constrain any god-type ideology we have and accept the right of any believer to design their own view of the Godhead. Although the subject matter may sound intimidating, given the fact that no belief will be proven wrong I suggest the Godhead is the ideal subject for deep contemplation.

The wisest minds of antiquity were purposeful thinkers who never truly found definite or timeless design. If they couldn't agree on one truth, I suggest this gives license to any thinking being to seek their own.

This book describes the process, book two builds your confidence, and book three, *Forbidden Philosophy*, presents several of my own more controversial Ultrathoughts. Some of these are oriented toward the Godhead and religion, but many more deal with science, quantum mechanics, anthropology, and technology. In a sense, my conclusions are a "forbidden philosophy." I believe the stuff I write even though you may laugh, scoff, or be angered by my views.

Many who know me are unaware of my specific opinions and may read my words as a criticism of their own views. That would be a misinterpretation. I am truly a freethinker who recognizes one's prerogative to think as they choose. However, I also reason that everyone should give serious thought to the creation of their narrative. Ultra-thinking is a type of purposeful whole-brain thinking that drives the thought process toward deeper and, theoretically, enlightened conclusions.

After completing the series, understanding the premise, and earnestly attempting ultra-thinking over weeks, months, and years, you will begin to create the best version of yourself possible. Whether you are oriented toward your logical-left or the creative-right side of your brain, when you can ultra-think to the point of building whole-brain Ultrathoughts, you, the thinker, will transform to become a poet. Your mind-myth story will then read as poetry. The poetry created is akin to a beautiful butterfly floating on the breeze of humanity, blessing the cosmos by its very existence. Continually ask yourself throughout the reading of the series, "Wouldn't I rather create purposeful poetry than a mundane story that simply reflects my innate mental inclination?"

Plato is credited with saying: to think is good for man. Let's push this statement even further:

To create Ultrathoughts is better for all humanity.

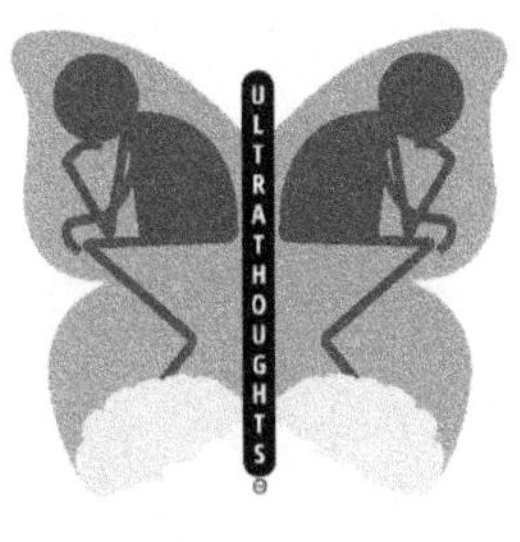

PART I

CHAPTER 1

THE LOGICAL-LEFT AND CREATIVE-RIGHT

You've probably heard of the curious fact about the two hemispheres of the brain. The left half controls the physical movements of the right side of our bodies, and the right hemisphere controls the left side. While most people find this to be an interesting but rather useless bit of trivia, there is a far more fascinating aspect of related research regarding how and why people think the way they do. Individuals tend to be either left- or right-brain dominant in their mental thought processes. Although neurologists remind us that this general rule of brain-thought orientation does not always apply, it has been documented in a healthy brain that the basic alignment of a person's thoughts can be measured as originating from either the right or left side.

This theory is not without its detractors, but research indicates that thoughts originating from the left hemisphere are generally grounded in reason, strategy, mathematics, control, and analysis, while those from the right are based on imagination, creativity, happiness, freedom, and emotion. The way one thinks manifests itself as characteristically unique to the individual and is reflected in their lifestyle choices. Even their choice of pet, and interaction with that pet, reflect their general brain orientation. A person who has trained a well-behaved dog is more likely to be a left-brainer than one who dresses their dog in a costume for Halloween—clearly a right-brain characteristic. Without intent to act otherwise, we all operate within our natural comfort zones.

Ultimately, we self-create the person we become. Fundamental to that person is our story of truth, our mind-myth. This aura of how you think reflects your very personal dogma. As we interact with the matter of the cosmos, specifically, physical matter, our self-created versions of truth are fairly standardized between us. We as individuals share many common beliefs: the roundness of our planet, the heat of the sun, and the wetness of water. However, when considering topics of the metaphysical (reality beyond the physical), there often is no such agreement among intelligent people. People frequently differ in their view of reality concerning issues of God, politics, beauty, and love. This circumstance concerning a self-created reality infers a conclusion: we each live an illusional truth of mind, a delusional reality. Our own mind determines our truth.

Some will find the idea unsettling; truth and your reality are merely mental constructs. You may even find this statement offensive. If you ponder the concept of a delusional reality, you'll note the supposition isn't offensive. Fundamentally, it is complimentary to the human mind—a tribute statement to the brain's complexity. Nor is the idea a slight of one's own belief in a superhuman force of God or the universal laws of physics. A delusional reality denies nothing; it merely recognizes the interpretive power of the mind. Any fact, faith, or belief may be validated as "real" if the mind allows. Since the mind is the judge, reality is not a physical thing but an illusion.

An illusional truth of mind, or delusional reality, is neither good nor bad. It is simply a feature of the human experience. Although ideology is considered a state of mind, ideological leanings can first be traced to the physical brain. Each individual brain is a unique product of DNA and the epigenetic process. Brains manifest noticeable orientation toward the left or right hemisphere. Individuals with an orientation coming primarily from the left side eventually create a bias toward believing that all reality is structured and just, while right-brained people tend to show an opposite inclination in assuming reality or truth is always adaptive and loving.

Given the background presented, you might assume that a right-brained person would be more likely to compromise. After all, he or she would tend to see the world as being more flexible than that perceived by a logical left-brainer. This assumption misses the larger point. The question of flexibility of opinion centers around the rigidity of thought, not the nature of the idea. A right-brain oriented creative is not necessarily more flexible than a left-brainer. Both are biased—the question is one of degree. Ultra-thinking deals with suppression of automatic leaning, not the promotion of either left or right oriented thinking.

One might assume the world would be a kinder and better place if we all thought the same. Kinder, maybe. But better? Not likely. The wisdom of crowds, or compromise for the sake of getting along, doesn't assure an optimal solution. What is most likely to urge one to creation of an enlightened truth? Whole-brain thinking often leads to better answers.

To be a whole-brain thinker one must struggle to free the mind of natural orientation. This can require significant effort. The mind can be a stubborn beast. However, through effort and practice, most of us can think just like the wisest thinkers of antiquity. To be successful, one must strike a balance between Aristotelian logic and utter absurdity. The ridiculous becomes organized and lucid in formation of an Ultrathought.

When I first became aware of my bias, I wore it as a badge of honor. After all, if I knew my ideologically laced truth was flawless, why not shout my revelation for the benefit of all? Many heard my idea of truth, understood any foundation I laid in support, yet they still just didn't seem to agree with my conclusions. Something was wrong. Thankfully I matured, coming to understand I wasn't so smart, and my critics weren't mentally deficient.

The problem was neither them nor me. There was not a definitive "our" truth. Others had a different truth in their mind, a truth that was worthy to them. But if I'm right and they're right, who concedes the point? The key to resolving this conundrum is to accept that the very first seed of your delusion lies in the physical brain, not meta of mind. Ideological leaning exists in all of us to one degree or another. Once this concept is accepted, the mind will begin to allow suppression of thoughts. Accept the supposition and watch your mind open to new ideas.

We all exhibit a bias to some degree, and it can be stifling. To overcome our bias and think from both the logical-left and creative-right can sometimes feel like mental gymnastics; a metaphorical stretching of the brain. Yet this workout is important if one seeks an enlightened and ideal truth of mind. This ideal truth doesn't follow in the shadow of our ideology; it uses the whole brain to discern the optimal. Once found, our enlightened truth re-educates our mind-myth as necessary and encourages further personal growth.

CHAPTER 2

OLD GENERALS AND OLD HIPPIES

Most of us go through day-to-day motions, not bothering to think deeply. We tend to get absorbed into the materialist lifestyle of the 21st century; there are just too many distractions. Distracted, we often lose focus. Our minds seem to exist on autopilot. Leaving our minds to their own leanings we tend to respond reflexively. A reflexive response may be accurate or not; regardless, it's going to be an ideologically tainted response. If we acknowledge that making thoughtful decisions is better than hasty ones, and we agree that past generations took time to think, shouldn't we do the same?

Ultra-thinking is the act of forcing the mind to consider deep contemplative thoughts all while actively suppressing personal dogma or ideology. This sounds easier than it is. We subconsciously build upon our bias leaning and hardly notice the end result. Your lifetime catalog of interpretation is your narrative story, which is integral to the person you are. The person you present to the world will tend to evolve as either a left-brained "general" type who lives in a reality of structure or a right-brained "hippie" type perceiving all that exists as ever-changing and supple. Such personal evolution is normal. Thankfully, most of us can be fair-minded despite orientation. Still, at the extremes, unchecked brain orientation can lead to the creation of a very dogmatic person who simply can't or won't even consider opposing points of view. These people, "Old Generals" and "Old Hippies," pose a challenge to fair-minded thinking.

My use of the adjective "old" is not meant to imply age but level of ideological self-absorption. While ideology tends to become more pronounced over time, it is obvious that younger people can be extremely dogmatic. Many young dogmatists are victims of both biological brain-leaning and indoctrination. Society, specific elders, and well-meaning teachers have a hand in our mind-myth creation. Younger people, having little experience in the world, tend to be easily influenced toward a particular point of view for a variety of reasons. As said view matures within a narrative, a rigid ideology can form at a very young age, creating a dogmatist. Whether the indoctrination is intentional or casual is irrelevant; the effect is the same. They often aggressively defend dogma when confronted with opinions different from their own. Because they are not wise enough in years to rely on intellect or the art of persuasion, they may have no choice than to use aggression as a means of making their point known. Younger people lack the life experience needed to be humble. Without showing a willingness to learn, or unlearn as the case may be, they would find it extremely difficult to ultra-think. Regardless, old, young, any age can be an old fogey in my use of the phrase.

Without doubt, chronologically older individuals have built a large library of personal experience and frequently present an aura of confidence. Confidence may appear to be represented by either pleasant enthusiasm or defensive posturing. Old Generals and Old Hippies lack true confidence, and what appears to be self-assurance is little more than bravado. Like a school-yard bully they are defensive. They haven't mentally justified their own professed belief. There is no Ultrathought in support of their truth, so they must be defensive. Otherwise, they risk showing the shallowness of their thought.

When old folks observe a nonbeliever of their truth they get defensive. Their ego is alerted and the mind is filled with negative emotions. There is no desire for understanding or opportunity to learn as a result. Those emotions may be expressed, but they don't have to be. Just as age doesn't matter, expression does not determine one's classification as old. An introverted personality type can be as ideologically immersed as an extrovert.

It is important to appreciate that a brain-leaning will always exist, but not every mind will become old, stale, and fully ideologically immersed. Ultra-thinking is a resistance strategy fighting against our tendency to become closed-minded as we become more self-absorbed within our own ideology. It requires awareness and is only effective if practiced. The strategy is more important today than ever. More individuals are becoming Old Generals and Old Hippies at younger ages. To be old in thought is to be ideologically blinded and create less than fair-minded thoughts. A stale mind becomes stuck in a pattern of thinking that creates a person who is a victim of brain orientation. Ultra-thinking is about creating visionary thinkers, not victims of reflexive thought.

With the rise of social media platforms and a very bifurcated press, I suggest society is fostering more generals and hippies at younger ages. Individuals appear to be enthusiastically expressing opinions in which they have become vested before they are wise enough to have thoroughly comprehended the issue at hand. Mind-myth could become old in theme, making it challenging for the thinker to enlighten himself or herself later. People seem to be brain-washing themselves without understanding the consequences. Old Generals and Old Hippies who do not possess emotional maturity, let alone true wisdom, are often rude if not quite dangerous to society.

My longest friendships are with individuals who I fear are becoming such old folks. In a sense, this shouldn't be surprising. I've always enjoyed speaking with people who take a stand, generals and hippies. No opinion is more entertaining than an enthusiastic opinion. I'm attracted to personalities that have a strong leaning regardless of direction. While a conversation with a person with a leaning makes for a stimulating discussion, attempting to have one with a person who is ideologically self-absorbed is frustrating at best.

In years past, many of us could have friendly but spirited disagreements. Now it seems more individuals honestly despise dissenting points of view. One of my oldest friends and more than one family member choose not to speak with me simply because they find my ideas offensive. Ideas, not actions, are the reason for our distance. I refuse to sit by and let this become the norm.

The particulars of our modern mechanized society are working to isolate us as never before. Too many political leaders, cults of personality, and profiteers across the globe seem to use technology to foster divisiveness. Divisiveness may be good for business, politics, and power brokers because it builds rabid enthusiasm, but it comes at our expense. Advances in technology are encouraging the consumption of media, goods, and entertainment, which magnifies the challenge at hand. People can customize their whole environment to meet their current state of mind. This feeds tribalism and constantly reinforces ideology. A significant number of individuals constantly fed in an aura of affirmation will mature into extreme examples of their tendencies. Two giant tribes of Old Generals and Old Hippies may very soon dominate all of society. Group members will be disgusted by the very sight of those who think differently than them. Of course, freethinking ultra-thinkers who advocate for the fair airing of any and all information through no filter whatsoever will be despised by each camp. Imagine our future more divided than we are today by a power of ten—a society of tribes who are at constant war and honestly can't empathize with any opposing opinion.

Within a lifetime of experience, it is hoped we each mature to be of sound, wise, and balanced mind, but there's no guarantee. Some people never seem to grow wise. They don't appear to have been able to profit from their years. Of course, many of the less-than-wise would disagree. They disagree because they either lack awareness, intelligence, or the ability to objectively evaluate themselves. Wisdom is different than intelligence or even understanding. It is the ability to profitably act given your own unique intelligence. A person with a low IQ score can certainly obtain wisdom, while a genius can consistently make foolish decisions. This is why it is often said that to be wise is to be able to recognize in your gut that you actually know very little. The Ultrathoughts premise fundamentally recognizes this mantra.

I frequently cross paths with individuals who are what noted author Nassim Taleb would refer to as the "Intellectual Yet Idiot." These individuals, whether young or old in years, delude themselves into thinking that their credentials offer manifest proof that their view is the only worthy view. I suggest the smartest who walk our streets are likely those without any degree. An intelligent person needs no designatory letters to prove their worth and has little interest in wearing graduation tassels for you or me to admire. Any accreditation obtained by a true genius is usually a happenstance of a quest for knowledge, not the goal. Letters may help your career, but they actually prove little more than perseverance. Some may obtain a PhD in a year. For others, it takes a lifetime. One is not necessarily smarter than the other, and each managed to focus long enough to do as instructed. Albert Einstein and Steve Jobs are among many who simply dropped their pursuit of a particular academic degree after having obtained the knowledge they sought.

Given my premise that we all live a delusion of our own creation, naturally I'm hesitant to disparage the beliefs of others. I don't enjoy labeling a person as an old-thinker. Old folks can be pleasant people provided you don't attempt to enlighten them. Furthermore, who am I to judge whether an old-thinker is right or wrong? I suggest we avoid a pattern of stale old ideologically immersed thoughts to emphasize my larger point: ultra-thinking leads to better conclusions.

Frankly, predictable thinkers give our society a certain stability. It's no secret that a group of truly enlightened people can pose a real challenge to manage, while old folks seem to work together quite well. Freethinking individuals often don't seem to have much interest in accomplishing the tasks necessary to make our society work to the benefit of all. Enlightenment may be the goal of any person, but if the world was populated exclusively by the enlightened, would the trains run on time? Humans living in a society live a much more pleasant existence when we all learn to compromise a bit. We need a certain number of people who stabilize society, and a few "wild cards" to push us to new heights. Isn't that a reality we all must share? The idea of ultra-thinking is to push yourself, not necessarily to change the mind of every person you meet.

For inexplicable reasons we are blessed with the ability—regardless of ideological leanings or dogmatic immersion—to discern the difference between Gandhi and Hitler. Even as a child we seem to be able to sense danger. I suggest this ability personifies human nature. We seek good, because we are virtuous creatures. Each day we awake in hopes of doing our best. Absent force or twisted anti-social dogma, we don't choose to have old and close-minded thoughts. Unfortunately, the tendency to be more immersed in our own delusion evolves through our subconscious as we continue to protect our historical narrative. We are self-interested.

Thankfully we are social animals, and a cooperative existence is also considered necessary. The benefit of compromise is constantly weighed against that of simple affirmation. Conflicted, we attempt to resolve the struggle by limiting our interaction to people that we agree with. Association with our tribe allows us the benefits of cooperation in a safe space of shared belief. Isolation within a single tribe contributes to the creation of old folks.

Regardless of our age, most of us aren't ideologically old just yet. If we were, we wouldn't be engaging in a polite discussion of ideas. While you and I can admit we are most comfortable with those of similar orientation, we aren't so ideologically controlled that we can't appreciate the lucid opinion of another—even if at first blush we deem them ill-informed or simply wrong. At will, we elect to hold our bias at bay. We can still be maddened, amused, interested, or absolutely fascinated by other opinions. They challenge our thoughts and stimulate expansion of our mind-myth. We can passionately defend our view and fairly reconsider when necessary. We have a chance to be enlightened by another.

If we convince others of the worthiness of ultra-thinking, we can help humanity avoid this growing challenge to our society. If we can appreciate all is a delusion, we can respect the truth of another. When we respect each other, we will continue to communicate and foster a healthier society. Ultra-thinkers aren't polarizers. They choose to live and let live, while they themselves seek to create the best version of themselves.

CHAPTER 3

CREATION THROUGH LIBERATION

Ultra-thinking is both a process and a methodology. It is a process in that there are steps involved, yet it's a methodology somewhat like the scientific method. The methodology can be summarized as follows:

1. Assume the nature of reality is unknowable.
2. Gain awareness of your general leaning.
3. Select a subject.
4. Disrespect your own biased opinion regarding the subject.
5. Gather information from all sources, particularly those you had previously failed to consider.
6. Using a liberated mind, contemplate your conclusion to the point of an Ultrathought.

Key to the creation of an Ultrathought is your acceptance of a basic premise: your reality is self-created and merely a delusion validated by your mind. To consider reality, a delusion does not deny the worthiness of any other reality, be it a physical reality or a truth broadly recognized by society. Your reality is not superior to any other truth but is fundamentally all that matters to you.

This supposition is designed to help you liberate your own mind-myth from ideological bias. The mind is both the store and structure of our own wisdom so adopted. That wisdom is intertwined with our self-created internal story. Recognizing that this story is a myth laced with your unique ideology of the world is a critical first step toward training the mind to accept liberation from innate bias. When accomplished, your narrative can be enlightened or even rewritten. When truly ultra-thinking, your leaning mind is liberated enough to seriously ponder the outrageous.

Ultrathoughts are interpretations, not absolute facts. In order for your mind to bother to ultra-think, the subject must be relevant. The gatekeeper in deciding relevance is your existing mind-myth. You and I aren't automatically intrigued by the same subject. I might convince you to casually rethink your stance on various topics, but I won't convince you to ultra-think unless your gatekeeper deems the topic worthy of the effort. You don't typically read a book on a subject you're not interested in, and you won't effectively ultra-think the irrelevant.

Ultrathoughts, your answers, are never a physical reality. They may echo a physical reality, but our interpretations are absolutely not real. They are ideas of weight yet remain self-created delusions. We can each view the same subject matter, objective evidence, consider exactly the same question, and yet come up with entirely different conclusions. This doesn't mean either of us is wrong. If you fully understand my point, you will recognize that in a sense we are each always right. The trick is to accept that one can be right, but this perception is simply that: a perception of truth.

Earnest ultra-thinking people will often disagree. The reasons are many. Surely latent bias or biological leaning is a factor, but it isn't the only reason two thinking adults come to different conclusions. It may be that two purposeful thinkers are simply interpreting data differently. One of them could be using a slightly different formula to analyze the same data. Of course, someone can have a bad day or even suffer from low blood sugar, which causes them to make a mistake. The reason doesn't matter. As long as each are truly ultra-thinking of fair mind, let them each have their own conclusion. What we are attempting to accomplish through ultra-thinking is not the creation of an absolutely correct interpretation. We are trying to create a whole-brain thought free from ideology. A lucid product of a liberated mind. Furthermore, we appreciate that an honest evaluation of the exact same physical facts, data, and open-minded approach can lead to different conclusions. We are flawed beings not perfect machines. We'll never change such a fact; however, we can improve our interpretations if we are willing to consider all data as we actively attempt to suppress our filter of ideology.

It takes practice to get good at ultra-thinking. Eventually it can become somewhat automatic, and you will notice a difference in your conclusions, but that may take months if not years. Assuming you are an ultra-thinking rookie, at this point you should attempt to build a record of successful application of the method, thereby convincing yourself the process is worth the effort.

At least initially you should be careful to select appropriate topics. I can't overstate the significance of this decision. The issue chosen should be meaningful to you and touch your core. I want your mind to realize the benefits of the process. Try selecting something you would be willing to argue over, an important subject that matters. If you're up to a challenge, try picking a specific metaphysical belief you have held all your life.

Once you have chosen your issue, make a preliminary exploration of your impression or casual opinion, all the while attempting to clear your mind of preconceived bias or the influence of peer pressure. Ponder a few minutes. What do you *really* think? Remember, that which you spoke or thought in the past is now meaningless. What your friends think is of absolutely no importance. If you tend to get emotional, resist the urge. If you tend to get overly rational, resist the urge. You are attempting to consider the issue without preconception in search of a whole-brain truth.

Ruminate this one question off and on for days or weeks while constantly listening to various opinions. After you've thought about the topic openly and honestly for a significant period of time, speak your truth to your mind. Now attempt to reconcile your value system and action to the truth you know in your heart. In brief, that is the creation of an Ultrathought.

Obviously, it's far more difficult in practice than in theory. If ultra-thinking happened all the time, our ideology would be largely invisible. Our mind-myth over the years will lace important subject matter with ideology often expressed as emotion. When you're overly emotional or defensive regarding a subject, that reaction informs you that you may have pinned your ideology rather than enlightenment to the topic. This isn't necessarily bad, but if you seek to ground yourself in an enlightened truth you must work to remove emotion from your narrative. Your goal is to limit both the emotion of the right brain and the logic of the left, facilitating a whole-brained thought. Let me give you a better idea of the process by using a concrete example that engages an emotional topic.

Consider this question: How do you feel about the death penalty being assigned to one who commits premeditated murder when of sober mind? Though you may have an answer within a few seconds, your quick answer is probably given without meaningful contemplation. Most of us have never been personally associated with the question. It's not a pleasant topic, so most haven't deeply contemplated their answer. Your answer was then simply an ideologically driven answer—certainly not an Ultrathought on the question of the death penalty.

The example provided deals with a heavy topic for a reason. Ultra-thinking on trivial matters will probably not lead to personal growth nor benefit humanity. Neither you nor society is truly better when we deeply contemplate our cell phone plan. On the other hand, you and society are improved if you ultra-think the death penalty and other weighty topics. Ultra-thinking would certainly help you make better decisions overall. Still, it's not worth the effort in every single case. Should you really bother to question your ideological leaning with all its drama just to pick the best cell plan? Ultrathoughts require effort that should probably not be wasted on trivialities.

When you commit to a topic, it is best to progress in stages. For example, let's again consider the question of the death penalty. Of course, if you have never formed an opinion regarding whether there is a special nature or primacy to human life, you are not ready to tackle the death penalty. How can one form a serious opinion on the death penalty if one has never contemplated whether a difference exists between human versus other animal life? For the process to be effective, you must first select and refine the appropriate subject.

Staying within this heavy subject matter concerning life itself, let's consider another question most would consider far lighter. Suppose you are a vegetarian and you want to engage in ultra-thinking about the ethics of eating various other animal life forms. The train of thought will involve you in a multifaceted ethical consideration of your place within the biosphere and the connectedness of all life. Is animal life as sacred as human life? Where do we fit within the food chain? Do we have a choice whether or not to eat another animal? The subject is still quite vast, possibly still too involved. The process of deep contemplation—ultra-thinking— quickly morphs into multiple questions each of which demand serious consideration. In this particular case it could be useful to further limit the scope and concentrate on the topic of eating chicken eggs rather than an actual chicken.

Our "life and death" target question has now been reduced to, "Is eating chicken eggs still in line with your professed vegetarianism?" Nevertheless, any question concerning life and death is serious and can still become quite complicated. How does eating unfertilized eggs from contented free-range chickens compare to eating the meat of a chicken? What if the chickens are not humanely raised but instead live under the horrific conditions of commercial egg farming? Do you truly care about the living conditions of an egg-laying hen? As you see, the egg issue has proven itself a worthy topic, though still far less encompassing than the decision about vegetarianism itself. Ultra-thinking will often lead to many smaller questions that form a basis from which Ultrathoughts develop. In this example, rather than mentally justifying a whole lifestyle choice—vegetarianism—we have shown it is imperative to break the topic into more manageable questions.

From this brief example you can see that the process of ultra-thinking can be challenging. As you think with purpose, you are reconsidering your own personal values, which can be emotionally painful. Ultra-thinking can create cognitive dissonance (the state of having beliefs that are inconsistent with your actions). Withstanding such a challenge from within requires one to be emotionally healthy or risk feelings of abandonment. Mentally challenging your professed belief in anything—whether it's eating eggs, vegetarianism, the death penalty, the sanctity of human life, or the sanctity of all life—might mean abandoning a dogma or fundamentally questioning your own core beliefs. What if through ultra-thinking you begin to question your core values? Are you living a lie of your own ideologically biased creation?

Though my question to you is rhetorical, I freely admit I've personally lived many lies in my life. I advocate for Ultrathoughts yet often remain a victim of my bias. I fail in my quest each day but shall try again tomorrow. Discovering and admitting this can be devastating, but it is worth doing. Peace of mind is a quest, not a reward. Take heart. Cognitive dissonance will subside when your actions start to match your rhetoric. If you commit to ultra-thinking, whole-brain thinking with the intent of liberating yourself to be the best you can be, you will walk with more confidence and peace than before.

CHAPTER 4

A PROCESS OF ENLIGHTENMENT

To be a thinker in today's world is to be a bit of an odd person. For a variety of reasons, people don't seem to like to think, and most of us don't actually attempt to become enlightened. Therefore, before embarking on an exploration of my premise, you should take a moment to contemplate your journey, its stages, and the likely response of your peers once they observe an enlightened version of you.

When you have an epiphany and ultimately change your stance on topics of importance, people will notice. When our mind changes, our rhetoric changes—as do our actions. That will draw comments from others. Trust me, the comments won't all be positive. Though you may be enthused by the prospect of enlightenment, be reminded that criticism by friends and family stings. It cuts to your core. Regardless of the hurt, don't argue or allow yourself to be defensive. Keep reminding yourself that all reality is an illusional truth of mind. Your reaction or lack thereof communicates to others your fervent belief in your truth. Enlightened thinkers in general aren't concerned about proving themselves to people who really aren't interested.

By the way, ultra-thinking doesn't have to involve a change of mind. The concept doesn't absolutely reject the idea that your existing truth is worthy. The process merely assumes your current narrative is skewed; therefore, it lacks objectivity. Your existing truth might be in line with an Ultrathought to come. If this happens, don't be disappointed. It is certainly possible that after ultra-thinking a topic for days, weeks, months, or years, you'll have simply reaffirmed your existing belief. Regardless, the process was worthy in that it clarified, justified, and provided personal confidence in your truth.

Whether you end up changing or confirming your existing truth is unimportant. Always seek to remain fearless as you ultra-think. Do not fear the creation of any truth. You are only on this planet for so long. As your years close, leave with peace of mind that you created the person you wanted in your end. You should be the author of your narrative, not a victim of reflexive thoughts. See and restrain your personal bias and engage your entire brain to create better thoughts. You are the only arbiter of reality, the person who is in full control of your truth.

I believe many of you will eventually create several massive Ultrathoughts. These could be life-altering if you let them. They have been for me and countless others. Regardless of whether the creation results in an epiphany or not, if—after creating an Ultrathought—a previously held belief no longer rings true, you still have a choice. Ultrathoughts don't dictate your action, simply your knowledge of your truth. You are the person you create. Live the truth of your Ultrathought, or live the lie of the old you.

Of course, I suggest you live your truth. I believe to do so is to live a rich and full life, but neither I nor anyone else can dictate your delusion. Do what you want. With that said, you should appreciate one manifest fact repeatedly deduced by the wisest minds of history. Our very unique species of animal evolved or arrived on this planet to live a positive and purposeful existence. To do so takes a bit of effort or we'll be random victims of circumstance. An organization of organic matter we call animals. Really smart ones I suppose, but fairly ordinary animals.

A contemplative life is not always a bed of roses, but it is the life we were born to live. We each make a choice every day when we arise: live with purpose and vision or not. So, do as you please, but never deny you are anything other than the person you create. This truth will set you free, even though at times it won't make you smile.

Arousing the mind from its slumber requires effort because over time we become so encased in our own ideology that our narrative simply discounts views that don't seem to fit. Our existing narrative determines the validity of a challenge. When we fervently believe we are correct, we will automatically reject an opposing view. Today's mind-myth is the gatekeeper protecting you from tomorrow's rewrite. If you are very confident in your own mind, then in effect you've instructed your gatekeeper to aggressively keep up the defenses. On the other hand, if you've instructed your mind to be somewhat flexible and allow other opinions the right to be heard, you are on your way to ultra-thinking. Open-mindedness is one way to think about the concept.

In the above narrative I used the term "open-mindedness." This and the terminology "whole-brain thinking" might be somewhat descriptive, but frankly, they oversimplify the premise behind ultra-thinking. Make no mistake: open-mindedness, thinking outside the box, and plain old whole-brain thinking in general are all good ideas. There are countless beneficial seminars with enthusiasts paying thousands of dollars to learn to "think correctly." While this is all well and good, and people can be trained to make better decisions, a seminar won't make you an ultra-thinking person particularly if you're heavily biased to begin with. The ultra-thinking premise has a key difference.

Unlike classical whole-brain thinking the ultra-thinking premise fundamentally assumes that your foundation, your very ideology, is flawed. The premise requires humility, and an implicit loss of confidence. Ultimately confidence will be rebuilt as never before through ultra-thinking, though the enlightened person must always remain humble. All knowledge is transitory in the end. Traditional whole-brain thinking typically seeks to build on your existing foundation, whereas ultra-thinking starts from scratch. Here we attempt to liberate ourselves from both biological leaning of thought, and any ideology self-created within our mind. All previous knowledge is assumed tainted by orientation and historical narrative. Ideally, to ultra-think we should contemplate as if we are quite ignorant of the particulars.

You've probably noticed it's much easier to learn than re-learn a subject. If your chosen topic is one in which you are an expert, the subject will pose a real challenge. As an expert in a given subject you probably have a rigid mind-myth protected well by ego. You can ultra-think such a subject, but it may literally take years. It is extremely difficult to shed both bias and knowledge at the same time. I started with a recognition of bias and believe that is the key to success. Once biasness was admitted, over time I came to recognize my contaminated view. I then trained myself to consider that I had been fed misinformation. I had been duped. When I became angry at my own truth, I knew it was then possible to engage both hemispheres of the brain. I was then a seeker. I suggest that when you feel anger and or sorrow concerning your subject you are on the right track. These are encouraging signs for the ultra-thinker. Self-doubt is an indication that you have lost faith in your existing narrative.

For this reason, ultra-thinking is best suited for issues critical to your person and our humanity. Ultra-thinking is hard work, stressful, and can be dangerous. If you join me in book two, *Godhead Designs*, you'll notice a significant number of philosophers who attempted ultra-thinking were for at least part of their lives ascetic. This is no coincidence. They became ascetics as they freed their mind of ideology, destroying their ego in the process. You are warned: ultra-thinking can be life-altering. Such a life lived within an organized society not accustomed to interacting with deep thinkers is not easy. Many philosophers of old lost themselves and their enthusiasm for physical pleasures. We know of them today only because they rebuilt an enlightened self from scratch. I suspect many (of whom we'll never read) destroyed their ego, became reclusive, and never bothered to put their thoughts to pen. While the unfettered mind is a superior mind that can create Ultrathoughts, it can also be a peculiar mind. I believe Gautama Buddha and Jesus were prototypical ultra-thinkers. They were each enlightened having confidence while maintaining humility. They would be outcasts in our society today.

We can't keep our bias suppressed for hours, days, or weeks by simply waking up and deciding to ultra-think. Your deep-seated ideology is who you are and is in control of your truth. Ultra-thinking demands you identify your ideology, quarter it, disrespect it, and keep it restrained with intent. To do so for a long period of time is not easy and shouldn't be undertaken lightly. You may not be prepared to learn your own truth regarding every important topic. Make no mistake; you may not want to reconsider your faith, political views, or moral stance on significant issues. Some people are simply happier left immersed in self-created dogma that has never been questioned. If you love every physical pleasure of life and cherish every compliment received, maybe you aren't such a good candidate for the journey.

Through persistence, it may be possible to derive Ultrathoughts from even the most stubborn brain. Admittedly, I've met some whom I doubt would be successful, the old stale thinkers. But who am I to judge? Every day thousands if not millions of people spend a few minutes in quiet contemplation; perhaps a few are peacefully sitting on a park bench at this very moment. Others use vigorous exercise as a means of jolting the brain out of stagnation. Are any of these people ultra-thinking? I suspect some are, but most would not be unless they accepted my two critical points: First, reality is a delusion of mind. Second, ideology must be suppressed.

Each person will have their own style of creating Ultra-thoughts. As much as I would like to give you more specifics, I don't know how you think. I've found what works for me is vigorous exercise while watching or listening to heavy subject matter. It seems when I'm physically weak, I'm better able to absorb alternative ideas in the background of my mind. For some reason my mental defenses tire along with my body. This makes it easier to come back and ultra-think subjects because my narrative has already been primed. It reminds me of when I was at the university and would listen to lecture tapes while sleeping. When tired, I'm fed the data without my ideological filter on guard. Then when I ultra-think, some semblance of alternative information has already been primed within my mind. This appears to facilitate a more willing acceptance of what to me would have been strange or illogical ideas.

Another thing that has worked well for me is contrasting the ideas of two people I consider brilliant. I've noticed it is difficult for me to consider the idea of a smart person foolish. Once I've assigned credibility to the author in my mind, I hesitate to disrespect even the most outrageous idea. My left-brain orientation rationally values the view of an authority once status has been granted. By contrasting opposing ideas from two opposing geniuses, I can remind my mind that they may both be correct. I used this method extensively in ultra-thinking the meta or non-physical. Book two is offered as a vivid example of this approach. Once you see brilliant minds disagree, you will agree with me that there are no absolute answers to the meta. Everyone uses their own set of facts, so we are each pondering the ideas from our own point of view. Brilliant people can disagree. If worthy ideas contradict, the failure is not the truths themselves, but the fundamental assumption about the very nature of truth.

As a means to help the ultra-thinking process along, you might want to attempt a little mind trick. Constantly remind yourself that all is but a delusion. Understand that your ego is married to your ideology. Your ego wants to maintain the assumption that your truth is absolute and not an illusion. By using the trick, you can allow the ego to tacitly admit a flaw in existing ideology through an acceptance that you weren't technically wrong before. You were simply a victim of the fickle nature of reality. Reality is but a delusion. Everyone is deluded due to the very nature of reality. If anything, you are uniquely enlightened. Ego is then rewarded, not scolded, because you, unlike your peers, have a deep understanding of the nature of reality and an appreciation that each truth is merely a relative judgement.

Ultra-thinking is an exercise of mind and you will develop your own style of execution. Whether you use quiet reading, prayer, meditation, walking, vigorous exercise, or you invent your own mind games is unimportant. You will eventually learn what works and will find the ideal method to encourage ultra-thinking. Like meditation, exercise, or even magic trickery, it gets much easier with practice.

When your ideology bothers you, you'll know you're making progress. This shows your ego is under distress as existing mind-myth is being challenged. Keep it up and you will start to create whole-brain thoughts. Actively suppress ideology and think as a person naïve on the subject matter; now you are whole-brain thinking in hopes of creating true Ultrathoughts. Continue the practice often enough, and you will create a habit of ultra-thinking. When a challenge is posed you will not immediately fall back on ideology. You will pause, sequester your automatic response, consider whether the topic at hand is worth serious contemplation, and start to ultra-think. This is exactly what the mental giants of history could do with ease.

It never hurts to revisit a topic when new information is at hand or someone makes a valid point. Part of my personal apprehension in writing is an acceptance that what I write today may not be what I'd choose to write tomorrow. Reality is malleable; therefore, my mind changes. There is no need to accept a single truth and live a lifetime in its shadow. Following the process of ultra-thinking, if the "truth" you previously developed no longer makes sense or can't be supported within the context of your personal values, it is time to reevaluate once again. Either your truth is misguided or your value system is out of kilter. Start from the bottom up this time. Strip your truth or belief layer by layer, all the way down to the fundamental question. You are then engaged in the process of ultra-thinking in a quest to generate a refreshed Ultrathought.

If you share your Ultrathoughts or present yourself in a manner that is different from what friends and family recognize as "you," some people will react negatively. You may be excited by your own enlightenment, but others may not interpret your enlightenment with such glee. Don't be threatened by their reactions.

Imagine one day a very close friend simply comes up to you and expresses their belief of a fact, which is completely different from the position you've known them to support for years. A cat person suddenly loves beagles. A Yankees fan turns up in a Red Sox cap. What would you think? Be it a view of politics, religion, sports, or the death penalty, you will first want to know *why* your friend had a change of heart. You're not interested in the details of their argument until you first understand what specifically caused this transformation. Your friend misses the nuance of your reaction. As they present their "new" truth, you continue to question their state of mind. "Why the change?" you wonder, not "Tell me about your truth." Your repeated requests for clarification will probably be taken as a personal attack, not a quest for clarity. We have here a "failure to communicate," as the saying goes.

Psychologists remind us that when we hear someone else explaining their position on a given subject when we've expressed no interest, our reaction is likely to be negative. An audience, unless they came to hear you speak, will hear your seemingly eloquent explanation of your opinion as a pompous and self-righteous sermon. Self-confidence is off-putting to most casual listeners. Self-confidence is offensive because it is viewed by a listener's ego as a threat to their narrative. Explanations offered that challenge the view of the listener create tension, and the more you talk, the worse it gets.

Anger is a defensive reaction often brought about by fear and uncertainty. If your audience is agitated, there is a very good chance they are hearing your message. They may even think you could be on to something. Something that they, themselves, have missed. Eventually, they may come to agree with you, but initially the reaction will probably be negative. Should you express your Ultrathoughts keep in mind that you may have seriously contemplated an issue that your friends have not. If friction arises between you and your friends, remember—not every argument is worth winning. It might be best if you occasionally keep your beliefs to yourself. After all, it is all an illusion anyway.

Of course, you may find that you tend to invite challenges to your ideas. You find you are no longer apprehensive about your principles. As an ultra-thinker your mind is clear. Your values match your rhetoric, and you are experiencing newfound confidence. While it's not your goal, you start to take on an aura not unlike that of a wise sage or spiritual leader. I promise you some people are going to be offended and seek to bring you down a notch. I urge you to remain steadfast in belief, but never hesitate to walk away each and every time it is necessary. Your detractors are entitled to their opinions, and you're entitled to a peaceful existence. What did Gandhi do? What did Martin Luther King Jr. do? They simply walked.

Though I suggest you reserve ultra-thinking effort for important subjects, broadly speaking, you can develop Ultrathoughts on any topic. Given my own personal history, I am attracted to considerations of the spiritual realm. Others may be drawn to topics of politics, finance, hard science, or the humanities.

Having refined the ultra-thinking process for decades, let me describe the flow in stages so you can get a succinct idea of what to expect. I am taking for granted that you have already accepted the premise of a delusional reality.

1. At the beginning, it's difficult. You're attempting to admit your own leaning and ideology. Most of us are unaware of our automatic way of thinking. It may help to simply ask countless questions and force the mind to listen to the foolish opinion of others. Sit back and let them talk. Listen as if you are an arbiter in a courtroom. Don't reflexively consider any response or judge the speaker. Truly listen—only then can you mentally compare the opinion of another to your own. At this point, you're not attempting to draw any conclusion, simply noticing the way you're inclined to think.

2. Once you can at least start to admit you have a bias, you can begin to ponder worthy subject matter. In doing so, you notice your reflexive or historical opinion. That is a good sign. When you notice your answer to the question pondered is merely your opin-

ion, you are on the right track. The mind is becoming malleable.

3. Next comes disrespecting your long-held beliefs. Although it's difficult and painful, you need to convince yourself that your current set of beliefs are likely to be wrong. Yes, you heard that correctly. Consider yourself probably wrong. This is the difference between ultra-thinking and traditional whole-brain thought. We attempt to accept the idea that we are wrong in hopes of further restraining our bias. If you don't believe you are wrong, you won't successfully restrain the ego.

4. Now you have some relief. You feel ever so slightly enlightened. It's been tough, but you're starting to accept or at least consider new ideas. You are gathering your information. Though you haven't settled your mind, you have started to free yourself from the self-created dogmatic fog allowing the outrageous a certain space within your mind. You will even recall various comments about you and the way you think that have been expressed by others. In the past you may have been described as this or that, and you laughed it off or vehemently disagreed. But now you start to realize that just maybe the criticism was valid.

5. As you contemplate a target for your reconsideration through ultra-thinking, the mind can become rather relaxed. You are liberating yourself from years of baggage. In a sense, an open mind is like a mind on Prozac. All's well, you're chillin' and musing, all while having a welcoming disposition. Sometimes, you really do start to just brainstorm for fun. Some of these

shocking ideas are funny at first, but then you start to ultra-think. Your mind suddenly becomes aware, and you say to yourself, "Huh, I never seriously thought of it that way."

6. Next, if you've selected an important topic, what was curious or funny now becomes more serious. Things start to get interesting. Your ultra-thinking starts to give you some hints of an epiphany. If you become overly enthusiastic, don't take the bait. Initial enthusiasm may not be an Ultrathought but your mind's twisted logic to wrap you back into your historical narrative.

7. The better result at this stage is not encouragement but anger and disappointment. This is the true sign you are on the verge of enlightenment or a major breakthrough. Think about it. Up until this very moment, with regard to your chosen topic, you have been misled by your own mind and/or those who indoctrinated you into a set of ideas. Who wouldn't be angry, ashamed, or disappointed? Very often, hints of true Ultrathoughts are negative emotions. All of these emotions are the result of your own ego. Push through. You are in charge, not your ego or outsiders who with or without intent misled you in the past.

8. With practice, you will restrain your ego and ignore your critics. When you do and come back to your topic, finish what you started ultra-thinking and find your truth. Don't rush the process. You are contemplating with sober and open mind, and eventually an Ultrathought will be born. You might find your prior position was exactly on point. On the other hand,

maybe you've been blatantly wrong, hurt or insulted others as a result, or worse. Either way, today you are enlightened.

9. If you truly picked an important topic and revised your truth significantly, you will ruminate. You will probably generate thoughts of regret. This is tough and very painful. You can't help but reminisce: the time you've wasted, lies you have promoted, ignorance and arrogance you've displayed. You must shorten this phase. The best way to do this is to continually remind yourself it is all a delusional truth anyway. If possible, try to smile at your own mistake; you are a person doing the best you can every day. The past is the past. Today you have produced an Ultrathought and have finally figured it out.

10. Reconcile your outward actions to your mind-myth or not; but you must be honest with yourself. If you don't at least consider reconciling mind with action, you're setting yourself up for some problems. Enlightenment is grounded in honesty, and without taking ownership of your created truth you will experience cognitive dissonance. Admit that only you elect to live a lie or a truth; regardless, it is a choice.

After your enlightenment, an Ultrathought of an answer, it would be a good idea to revisit and rekindle some friendships you've damaged because of your ultra-thinking experience. Remember, family and friends may not understand the new you. That's fine; they don't have to. But if a friendship is broken because of Ultrathoughts, you need to clear the air. You need to explain that you didn't break those friendships for entertainment; you did so for a reason. You sought a better truth. By taking the initiative to reach out to your confused friend, you are reminding your own ego that personal truth dictates reality, not pride or bombastic defense of dogma. Few can live a productive life without a healthy ego. Still, to live as an ultra-thinker you must keep ego in its place.

Those who can productively ultra-think for years are not victims of their own ideology, but creators of intentional thoughts. Intentional thoughts enhance both the person and humanity because they are fair-minded considerations of all ideas contemplated in a quest for deeper understanding.

PART II

CHAPTER 5

A CARNIVAL BALLOON OF REALITY

Ultra-thinking is a process that requires a degree of success in suppressing your innate leaning toward your logical-left or creative-right. The mind will resist such suppression because we believe the reality we have constructed and have built a personal ideology in support of these opinions. Our construction is our manifest truth. This is the greatest challenge to creating an Ultrathought: forcing the mind to respect all information in the face of an inherently biased narrative.

To help overcome the challenge, I previously spoke of constantly reminding yourself that all is a delusion. Since, mind-myth dominates my view of reality and we don't share our entire myth with any other person, it then follows that there are different realities. From my perspective, your truth is a fallacy or delusion of mind. Conversely, mine is a delusion to you. Speaking globally, any and all personal realities are delusions. We could then say, all is a delusion created by mind.

Encouraging your own mind to consider reality a delusion, a key facet of ultra-thinking, is far more difficult in practice than in theory. In my lifelong quest to explain things, particularly the universe and God, I started to think that it is plausible that some things are simply beyond our mortal minds. That statement may strike you as odd. To make the statement implies I actually thought I could understand the universe prior to my revelation. Of course, I was never quite so arrogant, but I am honest. I am a hard left-leaning thinker who was raised in a modern mechanized society dominated by science. Deep down in my subconscious, I had been indoctrinated to believe logic could solve literally any problem. Challenges of physics or metaphysics—it made no difference. Fundamentally, I assumed everything could be explained given enough thought or computing power. I recall years ago writing a thesis in support of the idea that problem solving is simply a matter of doing more calculations. Under such a very logical premise, any problem can be solved given enough effort. Any mystery exists simply because we haven't run enough calculations to solve the challenge. Eventually there would be no mysteries.

We are a product of our mind, and to a significant degree, that mind is a product of societal belief. I suspect that prior to creating my process of ultra-thinking, any reality I adopted was simply a reflection of the general view of Western society. Society itself has a kind of mind. This mind of society, or MOS for short, influences our view of reality in conjunction with our personal mind. The influence of the MOS can't be denied any more than you can deny your innate brain-leaning of logical-left or creative-right. They work hand in hand forming reality, or, more precisely, *a reality* for you. I suggest that most of us fundamentally assume that all reality is explainable, largely because of the influence of the MOS.

Of course, our place in the history of humanity is another factor in defining our reality. It should come as no surprise that a thousand years ago the manifest truth of reality didn't include ideas like search engines, air travel, artificial light, and clean water at every tap. This is our reality today, but it wasn't theirs a thousand years ago. I suggest it will be obvious to an open-minded thinker that reality can't be stable from the viewpoint of the individual.

Just to give you an idea about the fluid nature of reality, let me remind you of a couple of points. If you were to research a list of humanity's single most important inventions of the past several hundred years, you'd see "telephone" as one of the first few items on every list. Pause and reflect. When is the last time you purchased or installed a new landline telephone? Our world is changing so fast we barely have time to compile the revolutionary accomplishments before the list is ripe for change.

Noted scholars can't seem to even fathom the direction of the changes, let alone the specifics. Who even conceived of ride-sharing a decade ago? Search engine technology alone will change everything within a decade, yet no one saw it coming and very few truly appreciate its potential. Your doctor will be virtually replaced in less than fifty years! If you can train your mind to appreciate the speed of change in our reality, you will better appreciate its instability. You will then make progress toward accepting the idea that it must be a delusion. Only a vaporous illusion of reality can change at such speed. What will be the reality tomorrow? We can't even hazard a reliable guess.

Our interpretation of reality is profoundly fundamental to our daily existence. As a result, many will find it virtually impossible to remove themselves from such deep-seated biased interpretation. It is no wonder that most individuals choose not to dwell on the nature of reality. Reality is simply there. To think otherwise is to risk destabilizing your world.

A delusional reality has been very difficult for me to accept. I have been raised to believe reality is that which either has been or will be objectively proven by the scientific method. To deny this supposition is to fall outside the commonly accepted position of my society. My automatic view of reality is to perceive its nature as stable, inherently physical, and ultimately explicable. My reality, our reality, is then physical or material reality.

While the idea has a certain appeal, such a way of thinking is stifling and limits my ability to justly contemplate nonphysical (meta) truth. After ultra-thinking for years about reality, my very logical mind slowly became somewhat flexible. Though I will always be grounded in my indoctrinated view, I have made progress. What helped was reading, but I continued to run into the same problem. When pushed to the point of serious consideration, my mind became more stubborn, preferring its black and white view of the world. When pushed to express my truth, I denied that which my mind believed could not be explained by science. This meant I ultimately considered meta or spiritual truth fantasy and physical belief fact, despite my best efforts at re-educating my mind. I had two sets of truths, but one was deemed superior.

Most people who think like me would have been stuck, and frankly would have soon lost interest. I too remained stuck for quite a while. The difference in my case is I am obsessive to the extreme. Though it is not a characteristic I enjoy, for the most part I manage to focus my obsessiveness on productive tasks. This book series is a product of my obsession in a way, but before the books came a visual aid. The visual aid helped my mind move toward a willing consideration that reality itself is but an illusion of mind.

Since the creation of the visual, I have effectively created dozens of Ultrathoughts concerning truth and reality. My mind has been somewhat, but not perfectly, liberated from reflexive bias. In a way the visual is a kind of an Ultrathought itself. It has been tremendously helpful to me and hopefully will do the same for you. I call my Ultrathought about the nature of reality the "carnival balloon of reality."

As a child attending the state fair, my favorite thing was a particular type of carnival balloon: a balloon placed within another. If you recall this is a translucent balloon, relatively large, having a smaller, more opaque balloon inside. In my visual, the entire balloon represents all reality—a delusional reality of our creation.

Being comprised of two balloons in one package, reality can then be considered as two realms. I define these realms as the physical realm being the smaller interior balloon, and the meta or spiritual balloon being the larger balloon.

The volume of air within each balloon represents knowledge or beliefs. Note: I use knowledge and belief somewhat interchangeably. The knowledge is then segregated into physical knowledge and spiritual knowledge. The entire balloon is all reality, but types of reality are segregated by the determination of the class of knowledge or belief. There are two distinct realms or balloons in the representation.

The visual also reminds my mind of a not-so-subtle point. Though all knowledge expands over time, the interior balloon can never exceed the limits of the outer spiritual balloon skin. The physical realm is technically limited and may even be considered finite. Though its limit may never be fully understood, a limit does exist. The spiritual, or unknown meta, will continue to dominate all reality. Since nothing will ever explain the limitless or infinite, the spiritual will reign supreme. All known reality is ultimately subordinate to the unknown realm.

The skin of each balloon changes as the amount of knowledge changes. As a result, the line of delineation between them constantly moves. When the smaller balloon expands, the interior balloon encroaches on the domain of the spiritual. This represents an expansion of physical knowledge as mind makes sense of truth heretofore believed to be meta.

Though we don't often appreciate the idea, the delineation line between the two moves in both directions. Occasionally, what was once considered manifest truth or physical knowledge moves back in favor of spiritual belief or knowledge. A prime example occurred when we recently discovered that some types of particles (in quantum context) may in fact travel faster than the speed of light. We had accumulated a great deal of seemingly irrefutable scientific proof that this was impossible, yet it has been confirmed that certain particles do move faster than light. In the visual, knowledge that was once a physical proof residing in the interior balloon has been relocated to the unexplained meta, or spiritual, balloon.

Using the visual, I've come much closer to a willing acceptance that all belief and knowledge are permissible in my reality. Furthermore, I am reminded that the placement of knowledge in one realm or another is left to the judgment of the author of a reality. Just as a child believes in the tooth fairy with all her heart, I can believe otherwise. She may view her knowledge as a physical reality. She has her manifest proof—money left in place of a lost tooth. Years ago, she and I shared the same truth of belief in the physical realm. Yet today, she and I each live different truth.

My mind continues to lean left, and the MOS of the West continually guides my overall view of reality. However, by keeping in mind the visual, I've made progress and seem to be creating a mind-myth that is more flexible and willing to consider the truth of others.

Throughout the Ultrathoughts series, I speak rather casually of a spiritual realm being a kind of subset or even a dominant factor in your reality. When I say the words *spiritual realm* or even *meta*, I appreciate that the concepts are loaded with emotion and stereotype. If I were to walk down the street and openly speak of my view of the spiritual realm, just imagine the looks I would get. A few would listen, several would laugh, but most would simply avoid eye contact. While I am no street-preacher or Ranter myself, I respect attempts by believers to urge others toward some sort of spiritual awareness.

Before we can delve deeper into a consideration of what I call the spiritual realm, we must clarify the terms *realm* and *spir-*

itual. A realm is a domain. In my balloon metaphor your truth and even your view of reality are compartmentalized within the context of similar beliefs. The domain is not an actual location, of course, but an area nonetheless. An area, domain, or realm of similar beliefs exist with the label assigned by your mind. Your mind labels and stores those deemed worthy of consideration. Once labeled, the belief is assigned its realm. I understand the circular nature of the statement; still, once you appreciate that all you believe is all that is important to you as a person, you will get the point. The mind validates, labels, and classifies your truth within a domain of similar truth.

I suggest that the labeling of your truth is not as important as the process of labeling. All reality is a delusion, but if a consideration is not labeled it will not be part of your reality. When your mind deems an idea worthy of consideration, you are considering the idea as plausible. At that point, you've allowed the idea to exist somewhere within your carnival balloon. Further contemplation may move the idea to the physical realm, but absent any movement, the idea is an unexplained yet plausible reality. The spiritual realm, and for that matter spiritual reality, is any plausible idea not yet considered a physical proof.

If you truly wish to ultra-think and find yourself routinely failing to honestly appreciate the truth of others, the carnival balloon of reality visual should help. All reality is one balloon of self-created belief or knowledge deemed plausible. What is deemed physical or proven knowledge is merely a component of all knowledge you deem worthy of consideration.

CHAPTER 6

CO-OPTED BY SCIENCE

We have discussed two realms—a physical and a spiritual—but need to define the spiritual realm in terms of what it is not. The spiritual realm is all that is not the physical realm. Think of it more as an idea without material substance, a complex dynamic system that can't ever be fully understood or predicted. If the spiritual realm is worthy of consideration, you have allowed meta belief to exist within your view of reality. The spiritual is then the area of belief, knowledge, or ideas that the individual mind deems plausible yet unexplained.

The mind constantly makes decisions that are tacit attempts to explain information. Fundamentally, the mind prefers an explanation sought for every exposure or experience encountered by the body. Most of these explanations are derived biologically or subconsciously by the individual. The mind brings forth very few decisions within consciousness. These decisions may involve issues of the physical, for instance, "I am cold and need to find a coat," or meta, "Why is that person staring at me?"

When the mind brings forth something for consideration, in a sense the mind is using a methodology as it contemplates. It is believed, though not understood, that the mind is comparing, contrasting, calculating, and justifying as it attempts to integrate information within its existing narrative. Apparently, the mind uses a process similar to the scientific method.

Most credit the creation of the scientific method to one man, Aristotle, but it is doubtful that this one person was the very first to notice a process that is innate. Like other animals we have the ability to figure things out. Aristotle very eloquently documented the process, creating a methodology for use in logical deduction. Today we use the generic terms *science* or *scientific* to describe contemplative use of this methodology.

Science, according to the National Academy of Sciences, involves: formulating a hypothesis (a.k.a. educated guess); designing an experiment to test this belief; and collecting and interpreting the data.[1] From these tasks, a scientist seeks to disprove a hypothesis. Key to understanding science is an appreciation that we are attempting to disprove our presumed theory, not prove the theory true.

This methodology is fundamentally the same used by our individual minds. The mind is not actually seeking truth directly. The mind is attempting to bolster an existing mental hypothesis. This is done by gauging the plausibility of alternatives. When a new idea is deemed plausible by the mind, the credibility of our historical narrative is opened to further scrutiny. Doubt is incorporated into the story. On the contrary, if the mind validates no new information the existing narrative is reinforced with the passage of time. Our existing mind-myth gains confidence or doubt through analysis.

Inclusion of new information that fits within its existing narrative is preferred as it harmonizes with the past. However, if doubt is deemed logical by the mind, doubt is written in as a type of asterisk to our "truth." When a simple asterisk of qualification comes to overrule the existing truth, the mind changes.

Over time our mind-myth and its ideological view of the world present an aura of confidence. The confidence expressed—supported by habit, repetition, and even tradition—creates a unique dogma we each carry with us.

In a similar manner to mind, as science matured within society, the methodology of science came to present its own dogma.

Science has an ideology in support of its narrative. Science as a methodology then became as much a narrative as a method. The narrative reads: The methodology of science can justify or refute *any* educated guess. Therefore, there are no actual mysteries, simply questions not yet answered to the satisfaction of science.

This is now the dominant view of the MOS in Western society, and it is rapidly expanding in popularity across the globe. Understanding science as a simple methodology rather than a dogmatic set of beliefs can set the record straight. Unfortunately, most individuals don't bother to engage in deep contemplative thought about reality, and they certainly don't bother to understand how their fundamental misunderstanding about the nature of science clouds their view of truth. Science proves nothing. Still, this simple fact is lost if the mind elevates the dogma of science above the purpose the science. If the mind believes it, it is so.

As society continues to evolve and the MOS comes to further elevate the worthiness of all scientifically based assumptions, truth matures in a world inclined toward physical proof. This means maintaining any respect for the meta is becoming a challenge. We have the equivalent knowledge of the Library of Congress—our smartphones—in our pockets. We train our mind to assume all truth can be validated through use of the scientific method. An answer to any question is a smartphone swipe away. Only when an answer is elusive do we bother to contemplate why. Some certainly accept the meta as being possible or even plausible, but more and more people are discounting this alternative. They may not have enough confidence in their opinion to express it in open company, but they are coming to deny meta potentiality.

My concept of reality presupposes that perfect information doesn't exist for a variety of reasons. I concede that some things are adequately explained and others may or may never be. I suggest this statement is neutral, being neither anti-science nor pro-science. You may disagree, so I will take a moment to explain a particular point in my favor.

The scientific method, or science if you prefer, deals first with an educated guess and then decides upon an experiment using data to disprove the guess. I do ultra-think the universe is made of data, so the use of science seems very reasonable. I further believe data may in fact be rooted in the perfection of mathematics. Countless philosophers and mainstream scientists assume the same.

Science is certainly far more than data. We must decipher what the data is telling us, and to do so we must gather the right data. We should then notice a challenge. Data may be perfect, but if we are flawed in measuring or gathering data, we will derive an inaccurate yet scientifically based conclusion. This is one of the reasons the scientific method can never actually prove anything. Humans are the extractors of the data. Humans are flawed. We are therefore less than perfect when we extract, measure, and interpret said data. Given our inherent unreliability, one must assume that any results relying upon this data are tinted with the prospect of failure. We may deal with perfect data but will always glean imperfect knowledge.

Now that we've identified a critical flaw in the application of an otherwise fine methodology, simply for the sake of discussion, let's assume we have quality data measured with absolute precision. If you prefer, you can assume that a perfect computer rather than an imperfect human performed all calculations. Our information is then flawless, as are our calculations. What is the scientific method actually doing when applied? The scientific method is attempting to disprove a hypothesis or educated guess. When he wrote of his method, Aristotle took great strides for humanity, but he knew of the limitations of the process. No one, not even Aristotle, can disprove a negative. The scientific method simply builds a case for or against a supposition. It technically proves nothing.

A common example used to explain the purpose and application of science is the theory of a polka dot swan. One can perform experiments until the end of time, having access to all information, and never disprove the existence of a polka dot swan. Absence of seeing the actual swan proves nothing. All the scientific method will ever do is add credence to the hypothesis. As years pass having seen no polka dot swan, we come to accept as fact that none exists. Is this an absolute truth? No, and scientists understand the point. Does an everyday person bother to question their assumption of an absolute fact? No.

So far, we've only pondered science within the context of an educated guess. To say "educated guess" implies a reliance on logic. Can one make logical assumptions with regard to an illogical subject? Can one assume to propose a valid hypothesis of the meta or nonphysical? Expanding this line of thinking, we move to contemplate the meta in relation to the use of the scientific method.

The challenge is self-evident yet generally overlooked. If a methodology relies upon an educated guess whose worthiness is measured by physical data, the methodology can't be applied to a meta subject. In fact, the National Academy of Sciences agrees.

To paraphrase the National Academy of Sciences: because science is limited to topics of the natural world, scientific hypotheses can't be supported by supernatural causation; nor can they make statements concerning supernatural forces. Pause and seriously ultra-think that statement again. The most respected professional organization of science clearly states that when using scientific methodology, concepts of the supernatural (Godhead) cannot be considered, period. I suggest you internalize this fundamental rule of science. By definition, science itself must be anti-spiritual, and can only handle measurable data; that of the physical realm.

So what should we think of the reality promoted by science? The answer is obvious. Science will only deem a physical reality worthy. The hard sciences must neglect the meta.

If the mind of the individual accepts the reality of the MOS, which is dominated by ultimate respect for the scientific method, the mind will fail to deem a truth worthy that is not physical. All potential reality is then denied, and only a material reality may be plausible. The MOS in guiding a default reality promoted by science inadvertently limits the ability of the individual to justly contemplate the meta.

Many conspiratorial thinkers surmise this is a purposeful deception of science, scientists, Marxists, New World Order, or even satanic forces. I don't agree. I believe the dynamic is an organic and expected evolution of ideas contemplated by humanity as a whole. I take no offense at the dogma promoted by science because I see no purposeful deceit or mastermind behind the promotion.

With that said, there are a few specific individuals and groups that do apparently play the dynamic in a way to promote an anti-spiritual agenda. I could guess as to why, but I don't have a desire to accuse, simply a desire to inform. Information is the best defense against the ruse. Let's look at an example showing the dynamic of how science works to promote an anti-spiritual narrative within the mind.

The Big Bang, as you may recall, is a scientific hypothesis that depicts the beginning of our universe. Some describe this as the point of beginning. A "just before" state that some term a "singularity." All matter of the cosmos is concentrated in an ill-defined specific point.

Before the general acceptance of the Big Bang hypothesis, most scientists expressed confidence in an alternative view: the steady state theory. This theory did not suppose any actual starting point. It represented that all matter we know was eternally present, holding "steady." Although physicists didn't understand how the universe came to be in this steady state, they surmised that at some point science would understand why the universe existed as it did for time immemorial. Originally, they seemed to subscribe to the standards offered by the academy. These thinkers dared not attempt to explain the meta. Science had no quality math in support of its very soft hypothesis. Since the issue was so complex and basically void of actual data few even dared to attempt to disprove the theory of a steady state of the cosmos.

For several decades, various schools of science, having a sound methodology from which to work, showed a great deal of success building support for a variety of revolutionary ideas. Be these related to biology, chemistry, or physics, any hypothesis that stands the test of time comes to be considered more or less proven. That theme and momentum in favor of science helped promote a general idea that science could prove most any theorem correct. Science was starting to dominate the thoughts of MOS. The inherent limitations of the method would soon be set aside in favor of enthusiasm for the dogma of science.

Through its steady state theory of the universe, science had adopted the idea that the cosmos was there yesterday as it will be tomorrow. No one seemed to prove the guess incorrect, so the consensus was that the case was basically settled. To question the premise was to be dumb or simply ignorant of fact. The theory stood for several years with barely a hint of challenge. Though the theory didn't lend credence to a "first-mover" or God directly, in an odd twist it did seem to recognize an inexplicable superior or meta presence. Eventually, this in and of itself would be problematic, but in this era thoughts of the meta weren't quite so profane. In the early years of science there was a much better appreciation that certain principles of science were relegated to subjects having a quantifiable set of data on which to rely. People made a clear distinction between so-called "hard" and "soft" subjects of science.

In the early 1900s, Einstein arrived on the scene. He happened to make a handful of ground-breaking calculations that seemed to imply the universe was not static, not in a steady state. He wasn't particularly concerned with the steady state idea, a theory that had been around in one form or another for decades if not a couple of hundred years. Still, the universe appeared, through his math, to either be expanding or contracting. Wishing to keep his own mathematical model within the bounds of accepted classical physics, Einstein added a cosmological constant (also called the Lambda or λ-calculus) to his formula. This mathematical constant made his numbers work in harmony with the accepted steady state theory, the accepted dogma of science. Bear in mind that Einstein was not attempting to prove or disprove any theory regarding the origin of the universe; he was merely running mathematical calculations for other reasons. Simply to move his broader objective along within the bounds of the accepted theory, Einstein chose to let the dogma override his own mathematical formula. In an unusual twist, and as further testament to his brilliance, this same Lambda constant was used in the Lambda-CDM model of the 1990s to establish the theoretical existence of dark energy. But—back to the issue of the steady state—Einstein chose to adjust his formula in 1917 to conform to a baseless theory. In fairness, he was a young man at the time and couldn't necessarily afford to raise the ire of his more prestigious peers for risk of stunting his further professional growth.

Within months of his creation of the Lambda constant, other physicists came to insist the constant was not needed. They feared Einstein may have indirectly shown the theory wrong, but steady state was the only theory with any credence. To abandon this theory would be to admit a failure of the dogma. As early as 1917–19, Einstein's formula could have been used to disprove the hypothesis, but influential scientists chose to ignore the evidence. Within a couple more decades, observations of galaxies detected redshifts, which irrefutably proved the theory wrong. Several more decades passed, and the steady state theory remained the official explanation for the beginning of our universe despite specific knowledge that the theory was wrong.

One of the alternative theories to steady state was that since the universe appears to be expanding it must have had a beginning. This beginning of the cosmos was called the Big Bang in a tongue-in-cheek manner. This new idea could be traced to 1931, yet it took more than fifty years for the Big Bang to take over the long-refuted steady state as being the accepted theory of mainstream cosmology. Should you investigate this story on your own, you will find that the Big Bang theory was generally accepted by scientists during the 1960s. Still, I was personally taught the patently false theory of the steady state in 1978. This fallacy was promoted in top-selling texts for decades for no reason other than protection of historical dogma.

Of course, the idea of a spontaneous expansion is not without its problems. Frankly, just like steady state, the Big Bang is a statement of belief lacking any meaningful proof. One of the more obvious challenges to the hypothesis is that the speed at which the universe is expanding is increasing. Big bangs don't expel matter faster as they age—at least according to the laws of classical physics. There are so many obvious flaws in the theory that some prefer to describe the Big Bang as more of a statement than an "educated" guess. As you might have gathered, virtually everything we've been told regarding the Big Bang is simple conjecture. Nevertheless, science continues to promote the dogma that only science can provide answers concerning what is real. Your school-aged child is currently being taught a provably false theory, the Big Bang, for no purpose other than to protect the reputation of scientific dogma. In truth, cosmologists have no good theory as to the origin of the cosmos. This statement is an undisputed fact, yet most in our society have no clue as to its accuracy.

I devote so much time to this topic because I promote whole-brain ultra-thinking for the good of person and society, regardless of dogma, knowledge, or belief. When science, with or without intent, promotes self-preserving dogma under the guise of promoting knowledge, we are being misled. I was misled, duped, and am quite confident I am not alone.

Of course, the objective laws of classical physics are not our only tools for understanding physical reality. Quantum mechanics offers new insight, but because its results lend credence to ideas in support of concepts that point to things beyond the physical, traditional science often resists this field of study.

For example, scientists tell us nothing may exceed the speed of light. You probably still believe the statement yourself. But ask any physicist and they will tell you that when quantum superposition is considered, it is theoretically possible that certain subatomic particles do travel faster than the speed of light. Check any high school physics textbook, and you'll likely find the blanket statement of scientific dogma that the speed of light can't be exceeded. It is extremely probable that, once again, we are being misled. Quantum mechanics accepts the strange and predicts results in defiance of many laws of classical physics. In doing so, this branch of science finds a tacit harmony with concepts in defense of the spiritual realm, despite the mantra of science. As a result, once dogmatists are confronted with many of the apparent realities of the quantum, they quickly redefine the subject. When that fails, they often attempt to slander the whole subject, referring to many quantum concepts as pseudoscience. Trapped by their own dogma, these true believers have no other choice.

The cloud of dogma of science is ever-expanding as the method continues to build a catalog of success. Like your mind-myth, when the narrative of science stands the test of time, we gain confidence in the premise. Dogma and tradition work hand in hand to make a religion. We commonly think of religion as being spiritual or meta-based, but it doesn't have to be. Though originally conceived as a methodology, the idea of science has expanded. Science today is more than a method; it has also become a non-spiritual type of religion that promotes a rather unique dogma in direct opposition to any spiritual religion.

A natural dynamic of society and ego give the religion of science a key advantage over spiritual religions. Science, in some cases, offers objective evidence in support of its beliefs through mathematics and experimentation. Spiritual religions offer no such "objective" proof because they are fundamentally meta concepts grounded in ideas, not matter. People are unaware of this important difference and of the unique ability of this non-spiritual religion to offer proof. Society values objective evidence, and over the years people come to assume science is superior to spiritual religion in general.

This view is further bolstered by the gravitas of intelligent and respected academics who become associated with science. Prestige is transferred from these individuals to the non-spiritual religion. There becomes a sharp contrast drawn between the intelligent people of science and the rest of society. Our egos move us to seek association with the intellectual class, so as time passes more people will naturally migrate toward the religion of science.

Promoters of spiritual beliefs eventually become associated with people who are considered somewhat less intellectual than the scientific class.

Confusion about what science actually is will always be a challenge, which is why I continually spread the word that when a scientist attempts to address a meta topic, the attempt is a subterfuge unless the promoter explains the inherent bias of the methodology. Science, when addressing a meta subject, is simply a religion. It is therefore both a methodology and a non-spiritual religion.

As a non-spiritual religion, its basic premise is that only natural (i.e. physical) laws exist in the cosmos. In this book I use the term *naturalist* to describe one who categorically rejects any supernatural presence or influence. While this is common, the use of the term can be confusing. I don't use the word in description of one who simply appreciates nature or sees the Godhead as nature itself.

To be a naturalist believer is to have a worthy religion, but this religion is different than most every other. Unlike others, which have at their root a philosophy of the meta, the non-spiritual religion of science denies the spiritual realm. The denial is not meant as a slight. It is simply a feature of a belief rooted in a dogmatic set of principles in support of a method and not a philosophy. Naturalism, sometimes called Darwinism, represents that there is one realm; the natural realm of material matter. The entire spiritual realm is therefore negated.

You may find it strange to learn that many scientists—facilitators of the scientific method—aren't actually naturalists themselves. A thinking person of science understands his or her trade. Science first and foremost is a method. It evolved over time to become something more; a non-spiritual religion. Scientists in general, like the National Academy of Sciences, certainly understand the difference between a methodology and a dogmatic set of beliefs.

To have any meta belief whatsoever is to reject the non-spiritual religion of science. Scientists may or may not have spiritual beliefs but can't be naturalists while believing in a superhuman or meta type of presence. Of course, a superhuman presence is not quite the same as a physical—yet unknown—force. The superhuman force of God is a non-physical or meta force entirely different than a force having a physical cause. When a believer denies any meta realm, he or she is a naturalist by default. When an individual subscribes to the scientific method, the person is a scientist with regards to a given subject and may or may not be spiritually inclined. At the risk of confusing the issue further, polling of professional scientists indicates a majority are self-described atheists, not naturalists.

I urge everyone to be informed enough to distinguish between naturalism and atheism. These are two entirely different interpretations of spirituality. Atheism is a rejection of a particular or group of theistic beliefs, not a rejection of any and all spiritual concepts. A Christian is an atheist to a Hindu and vice versa. Atheism is therefore not de facto anti-spiritual though most spiritual people believe such is the case. From the perspective of most believers, his or her belief is the only worthy belief and everyone else is an atheist. A naturalist, on the other hand, is anti-spiritual and an atheist when compared to any spiritual or religious belief.

Just as philosophies became religions complete with traditions, the scientific methodology came to evolve traditions. Traditions, as they age within a group of followers, create dogma. Once a system of belief comes to be supported by dogma, history, and tradition, a religion is born. The religion of science competes against all spiritual religions.

CHAPTER 7

REALITY OF MIND

We comprehend our day-to-day existence through our direct experience in the physical world as interpreted through our own filter. This interpretation of a physical reality is ingrained in our mind, being automatically comprehended through interaction with physical matter. In contrast, creating a vivid spiritual reality within one's broader delusion of reality requires conscious effort. As a result, the treasures offered through an appreciation of the spiritual world remain a mystery to many.

Truth and reality must be mentally validated within the mind of the person. As you mature with your myth, you will eventually build a set of specific "facts" interpreted in a manner that supports your general belief. As beliefs gain root in the narrative of your mind, you will continue to filter out information deemed incorrect and allow information that confirms existing beliefs. Notice how very similar our mind works to the methodology of science. Existing belief (hypothesis) is held up against alternative information. Your mind is applying the scientific method to all information, not simply information related to quantifiable data.

The outside source of support for your truth may be science, a church, a philosopher, an organization, the MOS, pure math, or even whimsical magic. It makes no difference. We should accept that none will provide the perfect confirmation to anyone other than the believer themselves. Your mind-myth solely dictates results, not quantifiable data. Your mind exclusively validates a belief it considers worthy of contemplative thought.

It follows that there is but one single reality of importance to you: a delusion of your own mind's creation. This conclusion is the ultimate compromise. It denies no currently accepted laws of physics or future theory, and it welcomes the inexplicable results we observe through quantum physics. We are each deluded and reject no delusion of another. It is not a threat to humanity for us to honestly recognize this truth unless we become so warped as to deny our innate sense of good.

We each live in a delusional reality of our own making. Again, take no offense at my use of the term *delusion*. Substitute *illusional truth of mind* if you prefer. Metaphysical reality can't be disproven, so your own spiritual delusion is as valid as my opposing delusion. Think about it—at this very moment, somewhere on the planet a schizophrenic is chasing butterflies that are *real*. This is his reality of the mind. Reality comes in many flavors, ranging from that supported by an incredible volume of objective science to the wild meta-dreams of a madman. They are each part of a reality and are both at base a delusional reality of the mind. We should stop assuming the only reality worthy of serious consideration is that supported through *objective* science validated by our dogmatic mind creation. To do so is to deny what many believe is the most important reality to each person—your spiritual truth.

Unlike the hard sciences of physics, biology, and chemistry, soft science subjects like economics, sociology, and philosophy have no strict methodology. The data is often difficult if not impossible to measure and dissect. Scientists will use variations of the methodology in analysis of the softer sciences, but it is accepted that such discussions are truly theoretical. When dealing with philosophy in particular, a pure study of the meta, there is absolutely no actual measuring to be done. It is impossible to successfully apply the scientific method to philosophy or other topics of the meta.

If you can internalize this important discussion, consider yourself enlightened. The vast majority of individuals today never bother to ponder this dynamic.

The ultra-thinking premise recognizes all delusional realities as worthy from the perspective of their authors. One might leap to the conclusion that under my premise, a worthy reality is even one encouraged by the mentally ill or some warped societal norm. I appreciate that we interact within a society. With that being the case, we must come to an agreement on some basic rules having a structure of morality and acceptable conduct. Only then can we truly define what it means to act as a sociopath.

Any society has an MOS whether the society has three participants or three billion. In a dynamic nature, societal values are worked out and implicitly agreed upon. If I were a hermit, the standards of any society would be irrelevant. However, that's not how our species typically lives. To participate in a society, we each must generally adopt the standards of the group. If my own views fall too far outside what is commonly accepted and I choose to express those views, the best result would be that my peers would limit their interaction with me. The worst result is that I would be burned at the stake.

In further consideration of an illusion of mind or delusional reality some may say, "You can think what you want, but if that objectively based thirty-ton truck of reality smacks you on the freeway, you will soon learn which reality is most important." That's true, but I should stress to the reader that I specifically framed my discussion under the topic of metaphysics, not the material science of physics. In everyday physical experience there is tangible substance, or matter, which we tend to universally perceive. This is our physical reality having characteristics I too generally accept as being material. Yes, that truck will kill me as an individual. However, reality is what your mind tells you is true, regardless of any objective proof.

I wish to highlight how our perception of the so-called facts of science guide all truth. Let's consider a subject far more physical than spiritual. The earth is round. Certainly, that fact is objectively proven by science. The statement is an objective truth. Right? Actually, it is not. Our planet is not perfectly round. The earth has a noticeable bulge near its equatorial region and is squashed at its poles. Reality or truth is subject to one's interpretation of the concept of round. Furthermore, we must appreciate that all theories or hypotheses of science—in this case, the earth is round—are subject to something called the domain of applicability. If one's domain in consideration of the question of roundness was "general," then the statement was true. But, if the assumption behind the statement existed under a more precise definition of roundness, the declarative statement about the earth is false. As you see, the valid reality is not an actual physical reality. Truth, particularly truth deemed objective, is subject to a specific domain of applicability. The key in determination of the truth was the delusional reality with its biases and domains all being products of the mind.

This basic earth example does not represent the use of simple wordplay. Everything regarding objective science can be scrutinized along the same line of ultra-thinking. We use language interpreted by the mind to represent a given reality. Language is used in the representation of somewhat mutually agreed upon facts. Even highly objective technical facts, like the shape of the earth, are all filtered through your personal mind-myth. You use knowledge, uniquely described through your own comprehension of language and symbols, to refine a truth. From your personal interpretation you develop your own delusional reality.

Language, another construct of the mind, is not objective either. It is merely used as a tool to build your mind-myth. Your use of language is customized into your own story as it is being reinterpreted continuously. One person's common use of a curse word might be meaningless to many but highly offensive to another. The same word, with different perceptions of its meaning, results in drastically different mind-myth construction. Even one's voice inflection or additional tone placed on a single word of language can completely change the meaning of the most seemingly obvious statement. A statement made in common speaking tone versus one made in a sarcastic tone completely changes one's internal story. The mind's interpretation of language and symbols is dominant—not objective science.

Until these fundamental concepts—the mind is dominant, and objective proof of science proves very little if anything—are internalized, educated members of our post-modern society will continue to deceive themselves. They will inadvertently relegate any belief in the spiritual to second-class status, or worse still, they will fail to contemplate the meta at all. The way this subconscious mental bias is overcome is to accept that all reality is equally worthy of consideration whether of a spiritual or physical nature. If all reality is worthy of consideration, it then follows that all reality, in a sense, is delusional.

Psychologists remind us that awareness of bias is the single most effective way to overcome its influence. While a particular reality concerning matters of the physical realm may be bolstered by objective science, one must always keep in mind that such proof is subject to revision. One should not automatically elevate truisms of the physical above those of the spiritual. Should one be bound to accept as reality only a truth supported by objective science, he or she will continue to be limited mentally. One whose personal values and associated mind-myth are bound in the physical sciences cannot fully appreciate the spiritual realm no matter how much deep contemplative thought is mustered.

In other words, scientific so-called truth and spiritual belief are each nothing other than a faith. Shouldn't that be taught in science class? For example, as recently as the early 2000s, the facts of science told us there was absolutely no water on Mars. Those who internalized the statement without a hint of skepticism would probably assumed the issue was settled and might have further believed there was absolutely no chance of ever finding life on that planet given their belief that there was no water.

Once a belief is established, a position has been staked out. A position is worth defending. When that occurs, the individual is vested in the truth and is reluctant to forfeit the position. Such a belief about water on Mars would likely bolster an overall mind narrative that there is little chance life exists beyond our planet. Yet, in 2017, many of the same scientists who had for years stated there was no water on Mars confirmed through new and improved science that it is plausible that oceans of water could exist a few meters below the surface of the planet. Frankly, this is one of the countless examples of the failure of science. And I do mean quite bluntly, failure. This example probably results from sloppy science, a simple error. However, science often fails us not because of error but deception in defense of dogma. I could provide a litany of examples, but many of my favorites concern the cosmos.

It is calculated by cosmologists themselves that they can only explain around four percent of the matter in our universe. This means that cosmologists, likely our best and brightest scientists, don't even know what makes up over ninety percent of the universe. How could these same individuals offer a serious proposal on the origin of physical existence if they don't even understand what it's made of? Some support theories that this missing matter will be somehow observed through studies of dark energy and dark matter. Unfortunately for their theory, neither of these have been definitively confirmed anywhere, ever. Scientists once again simply hypothesize or believe such to be the case, and we're inundated with this purported wisdom of science. Let that soak in for a moment; cosmologists don't even know what it is they are attempting to explain. Yet rather than simply stating that science has no sound idea as to the origin of the cosmos, we are indoctrinated to internalize unfounded conjecture. As was the case in the steady state and Big Bang theories, over time the stated conjecture morphs into a truth of the MOS, and individuals don't bother to question the dogma.

To be perfectly clear, I am not a believer in notions of solipsism—the circular epistemological position that nothing material exists. Furthermore, I respect the non-dualistic position you may hold. If you are a naturalist, spiritual believer, or whatever, this is not my concern. When I criticize science while advocating for concepts such as a delusional reality, my intent is not to imply there is no physical reality based on objective proof. Physical reality can be scientifically proven, at least for a while. What is being stressed is that vaporous thought, wrapped in scientific pomp having little or no support, is routinely considered to be buttressed by objective measures, thereby misleading one's mind-myth and further pushing a bias in favor of science itself. This ultimately has a negative influence on the quality of one's personal delusional reality as it trains the mind to deny any plausibility of a meta. Given the prestige assigned to scientifically based truth in general, far too often once a belief is accepted within the mind, the mind itself shuts off further consideration. Ultra-thinking is not allowed in a closed mind.

My ultra-thinking leads me to conclude the day of reckoning is at hand. Anecdotal evidence informs me that those who are spiritually inclined seem to be becoming more so, while those who reject spiritual notions are also increasingly confident in their position. Very soon, spiritual believers will come to realize that while they see a coming age of enlightenment, their view is a product of self-immersion within a society of like-minded thinkers. Surveys consistently show the secular view of the MOS is overwhelming humanity in general. Soon society will be split between those who loathe science and those who loathe the very idea of a meta realm. The entire challenge is being rooted in a fundamental misunderstanding about the very nature of reality. The only reality that truly matters is a product of the mind. Reality of the masses will ultimately be a reality with no notions of the Godhead.

This train of thought leads us to ultra-think questions regarding how much longer the majority of people will value meta concepts as they do today. If knowledge continues to expand, isn't it logical to assume that eventually knowledge of the physical realm will have engulfed all of the carnival balloon in my previous analogy?

My response is to remind the thinker that although we perceive the knowledge of science as objective, in truth it is not. Scientific truth changes. If this truth changes, then it stands to reason that at some point it was simply wrong. Pushing this ultra-thinking further, the so-called objectivity in which you placed faith was nothing other than a personal delusion at best.

If the preceding defense of my Ultrathoughts is a bit too philosophical, then let's talk math. The vastness of the universe defeats any complete understanding. Be reminded of some very basic math: infinity used in any formula leads to an infinite product. If the universe is infinite, or itself consists of a multiverse, no formula or knowledge will result in any product other than infinity. A physical, yet infinite universe will remain a mystery.

Admittedly, we don't know if the universe is infinite or finite yet expanding, but either way, the numbers involved are simply beyond practical calculation. In concept, by making such a statement, I'm accepting a fundamental rule of science: domain of applicability. All hypotheses of science assume a boundary of application. When I say "beyond practical calculation" I am merely adopting the scientific premise of limitation.

We commonly throw around terms like a billion or even a quadrillion, but we truly cannot comprehend these numbers. As an example, let me remind you that the running of calculations involving something as relatively basic as a hurricane trajectory defies even our most advanced technology. Can anyone then honestly believe humanity would possess a technology that could accurately model everything? Not simply most everything, but literally everything. Every single motion or event in a perfectly quantifiable predictive model. That is what would be required for science to dominate the spiritual realm. Ultra-think that logically for a moment. Could we ever predict the path taken by every grain of sand in the Sahara Desert (a large, but finite number) during a dust storm? Now understand there are trillions upon trillions of atoms in our solar system. Could we ever predict the path traveled by every atom in our solar system? How about the galaxy or the cluster of galaxies to which we belong?

No doubt the reality of the spiritual realm will be captured by more knowledge. One day our artificial intelligence technology or quantum computer-driven machines will be so advanced they will not even bother telling us lowly humans what they are doing. Despite my obvious bias in making these statements, let's ultra-think the position of those who truly believe we will comprehend everything about everything at some future date. Let's give science the benefit of the doubt as we think from both sides of our brain in hopes of truly creating Ultrathoughts. We will now seriously ponder the outrageous.

In the interest of whole-brain ultra-thinking, we'll assume artificial intelligence can run calculations beyond our wildest comprehension. Artificially intelligent machines are then used to design and build a perfect source of artificial intelligence. The loop is truly glorious and the king of all AI is on the verge of saying, "God is finally dead, and proof will soon be had!" To make it a bit easier, we'll also assume the universe, not simply the galaxy, is fixed in terms of its number of atoms and subatomic particles at a given point in time. Through brute force, some future machine is not intimidated by the calculations required to plot the course of every subatomic particle in a finite universe. The master of the physical realm itself would then theoretically know everything about itself.

Now ultra-think further. If everything is known, by my definition this would negate the spiritual realm. All paths are now known being reduced to a solvable formula. But, wait. To truly understand "everything" means to be able to calculate all in the universe including its function. Cosmologists and mathematicians remind us that the universe itself, whether finite or not, includes complex systems. Complex systems involve something called open systems, meaning the systems are constantly in flux being subject to an everchanging set of variables and rules. The particles can be fixed and finite, the data can be perfectly measured, but the equations will never be static. Complex systems, as a result, can't be predicted with any meaningful degree of certainty. Questions involving complex systems—for instance, the path of a feather in a hurricane (a common reference used to refer to this paradox)—can't be calculated under any circumstance without closing the system—a fundamental impossibility for a functioning complex system. A finite system is not necessarily a closed system. Even if the universe itself was finite, since it includes systems there will always exist fundamentally unsolvable problems. An unsolvable problem infers the incalculable spiritual realm. We're back to where we started; the unknown will always exist. The spiritual realm can never be completely ruled out.

The more interesting and probably more crucial question is whether humanity will continue to acknowledge the dominance of the spiritual over the physical realm. Or will we be so driven by the combined force of ego and faith in knowledge that any sense of the spiritual realm would be overwhelmed within our minds? Should that happen, what impact would it have on us as a species?

CHAPTER 8

REAL ISN'T REALLY

Accessing the physical realm is automatic for all carbon-based life, be it a single-celled organism or a human being. The physical world of atoms and molecules, large things, is pretty well understood, I assume. We believe, as incorporated within our delusional reality, that a physical reality is present. As a matter of scientific conclusion, physical reality exists. We don't pass through walls, you aren't simply imagining the presence of your skin, and your feet touch the ground. While it is true that, technically, physicists remind us that in strict terms nothing is solid, in our practical experience, matter—the physical substance of atoms—exhibits characteristics of being a specific state: either solid, liquid, or gas. The science of classical physics in just the last two hundred years has explained a tremendous amount regarding physics, but the laws of classical physics have not been proven applicable to the quantum world. The quantum in context here means discrete packets of energy, or small things, like certain subatomic particles far smaller than any atom.

Most physicists, when considering the nature of reality, believe in using a reductionist approach. This method operates under the assumption that all the cosmos can be explained through the current set of fundamental laws of physics. The same laws we use to explain larger things like atoms and molecules are presumed applicable to the quantum. However, despite an unfathomable amount of time and money being spent, this idea hasn't been proven.

Building a more thorough understanding of the nature of physical reality through drilling down into the laws of physics is not necessarily enhancing our comprehension significantly. In many ways, the attempt to use a reductionist approach produces more questions than answers. Still, physicists in general tend to believe that given enough time and calculating power, all will be eventually interpreted by using the same basic laws. It is worth remembering that inherent in our discussion is the premise that science itself allows no consideration of the supernatural or anything that may be considered metaphysical. To a certain extent, physicists have little choice but to apply a reductionist approach to questions of the quantum.

I suggest that when scientists attempt to study the quantum they might be considering the line of distinction between the spiritual and physical realms of reality. That dividing line between the known and the unknown continues to shift. These shifts should remind the scientist that the challenge posed lies outside the capability of the laws of classical physics. Having hit some seemingly insurmountable challenges, possibly they should abandon the reductionist approach altogether. In doing so they can direct their efforts specifically towards the branch of science known as quantum mechanics in an attempt to better understand reality. Many of those supporting continued attempts at using traditional models are reluctant to move forward toward an unabashed study of quantum mechanics because this newer science tends to morph into topics of a metaphysical nature.

The quantum world as represented by several mathematical models of quantum mechanics is associated with genuinely bizarre theories and unexplainable results that appear to objectively support conclusions of a meta tone. Traditional physics, pursuant to the preservation of creed, considers the acceptance of an unknown product to be a bridge to a metaphysical or spiritual explanation. To some, even to acknowledge the slightest possibility of a metaphysical solution is to breach the very definition of science. This "science first and only" belief or dogma locks both science and the scientist in a box. The dogma of science insists science itself can never cede ground or contemplate the metaphysical, yet it is becoming quite obvious to any ultra-thinking person that the laws of classical physics can't explain everything in the universe. The reductionist approach fails to appreciate the concept of the domain of applicability that science itself invented regarding a hypothesis. A reasonable explanation of the quantum realm (small things) may simply fall outside the domain of applicability with regards to the laws of physics. In such a case, a newer model, a revolutionary model of reality, may prove necessary if we are ever to explain the quantum, and if said investigation leads us to inadvertently add credence to concepts that are metaphysical, so be it.

A person indoctrinated into the religion of science, or simply very inclined to give deference to its dogma, would be well-served to explore the quantum world. To even begin to conceptualize this complex science you need to do some ultra-thinking, and few will ever gain anything more than a casual understanding of the concepts involved. Nevertheless, I believe everyone would benefit from devoting some time to this subject. My Ultrathoughts lead me to believe that the formulas and proofs involved in this weird science just may be providing some clues in support of my belief in the spiritual realm.

Formulas and scientific proof provided through the study of classical physics, the equations of large things, frequently break down when applied at a subatomic level. We need the tools and formulas provided by quantum physics. One of the more exciting results in the field was the proof of a theory that predicted the existence of gravitational waves, a quantum phenomenon. Because of successes like this, many cutting-edge scientists assert that just as the physical realm had been explained through classical physics, the science of the quantum world will be reasonably understood within the next decade using ideas of quantum mechanics. In doing so an implicit admission of the meta is incorporated within truth. A manifest or objective truth is not fundamentally required to explain reality. While this premise will not fully explain the spiritual, its study will lead to a better understanding of what may be understood by humanity.

Here is a mere snapshot of a handful of the strange scientific results that fly in the face of the laws of classical physics:

- Within the context of particular quantum experiments it appears the speed of light may be exceeded.[2, 3]
- Simply observing a particle creates a reality that appears to be predestined before the observation.[4]
- Particles spontaneously appear instead of moving from point A to point B.[5]
- Particles that had been separated continue to influence each other from a distance, instantaneously and through no means of communication that can be explained.[6]

Moore's Law, which predicted the exponential growth of computing power, may lend credence to the idea that the use of artificial intelligence in the study of quantum mechanics, not classical physics, may adequately explain the spiritual realm. Note I said *adequately*, not *fully*. Could this ultimately lead to an understanding or even proof of what I heretofore have called the unknowable spiritual realm? Like many, I don't believe we will ever fully grasp the spiritual, but we could adequately understand. Given all the computing power in the universe—enough to predict the path followed by every atom of reality—even our best artificial intelligence would not generate enough insight to provide a perfect explanation of the Godhead (or however you choose to describe the ultimate perfection of the spiritual). We should, however, hold out hope that further study of quantum mechanics might provide insight into what may be the shadow cast by the spiritual world. We can never fully comprehend, but we may glean something valuable in our pursuit of an understanding through the production of Ultrathoughts.

I should take a moment to address countless books written either in favor of or in opposition to spiritual concepts. Many if not most of these books are fascinating as they give us a glimpse into Ultrathoughts derived by some extremely thoughtful minds. I believe I've read dozens, if not more than a hundred of them. However, there is often an obvious oversight when an author attempts to prove or disprove the spiritual realm exclusively through use of objective measures of science. I dare say when this occurs it is probable the book will miss its mark.

If you think through the dynamic, it is not possible to derive an ultimate conclusion in assessment of the spiritual through the use of physical science. When this is attempted, with all due respect, the author's ultra-thinking process might be interesting and informative, but the value of the ending Ultrathought itself is debatable. I suggest that *proof* of the meta is only found within the mind of the seeker.

Science might lend credence in support of the idea, but in the end to confuse objective proof of the meta with objective facts of physical science is to risk confusing the audience. I suggest that at some point it comes down to this: Either you have a faith in the meta or you don't. Never be afraid to simply say; "Yes, I believe, because I think it is true." It is your right to choose your spiritual belief. Forget what the rest of us think or even ultra-think. Some will criticize; I may criticize, but we are nothing to you. I write with deference to the learned and the dull, but neither are anything to me in the end. Ultra-thinkers must be fearless in telling what they really believe.

PART III

CHAPTER 9

THE ORIGIN OF US

Although the math behind the science continues to change, and cosmologists can't decide if there is one universe or an infinite number, the supposed age of our cosmos in relationship to our species, *Homo sapiens*, is shocking.

- The universe is said to be about 14 billion (14,000,000,000) years old.
- The Earth is 4.3 billion (4,300,000,000) years old—roughly 30% of the age of the universe.
- Organic cell life is 2.1 billion (2,100,000,000) years old—15% of the age of the universe.
- Animal life is 590 million (590,000,000) years old—4% of the age of the universe.
- Dinosaurs came into existence 230 million (230,000,000) years ago—1.6% the age of the universe.
- Great apes—Hominidae—are 15 million (15,000,000) years old—1.1/1,000th the age of the universe.
- *Homo erectus*, a human-like ape of the hominins group, first walked 1.9 million (1,900,000) years ago—1.4/10,000th the age of the universe.

- *Homo sapiens* is thought to be more or less 250 thousand (250,000) years old—1.8/100,000th the age of the universe.

Because the numbers are nearly beyond comprehension, let's add some context. We'll now assume the universe, all that makes up the cosmos, is 365 days old.

- The universe is 365 days old.
- The earth is 112 days old.
- Organic cell life is sixteen days old.
- Great apes (Hominidae) are nine hours old.
- *Homo sapiens* is ten minutes old in comparison: 7/1,000ths of one day in that 365-day year.

To put a few actions of mankind in perspective using this same one-year analogy for the age of the universe, we'll convert our year into seconds. A year then consists of 31,557,600 seconds.

- The Great Pyramid of Giza in Egypt was built in the last ten seconds of that 31,557,600 seconds in the span represented as the universe.
- The Roman Empire fell no more than three seconds ago.
- The United States was formed in the last half-second of the 31.5 million second representation of the age of the cosmos.

Anthropologists are in general agreement that *Homo sapiens* (a.k.a. modern humans) originated in sub-Saharan Africa roughly 250 thousand years ago. Our species started to expand its range beyond this geographic homeland some seventy-five thousand years later. Most of what were sporadic migrations likely consisted of small wandering bands of modern people who looked like us. We can assume these trips tended to occur in times of environmental stress. Very few descendants of these early travelers survived, but some did and maintained a traceable DNA lineage we can see today. It is theorized that these marginally successful migrations eventually resulted in multiple, yet very small, subpopulations that slowly gained a foothold in Europe, Asia, the South Pacific, and Australia. Being isolated from the broader population of the sub-Saharan humans, these early *H. sapiens* subgroups developed regional variations like fair skin, shorter stature, pointed noses, or even pockets of fat near the eyelids. Evolutionary theory tells us these regionally advantageous gene mutations served a specific purpose and were inherited by subsequent generations. We're informed that the races we observe today are a result of the success of these smaller congregations of people.

Significant numbers of *H. sapiens* are believed to have migrated out of the plains of southern Africa around seventy-five thousand to fifty thousand years ago. Without this last major migration some speculate that just like so many other hominins, modern humans may have become extinct. The impetus for this migration is theorized to be global climate change, although this is pure speculation. Geologists tell us that for reasons not fully understood, the climate of our planet periodically changes significantly. A particular cycle of climate moderation in the region of the Sahara Desert may have allowed modern people to migrate in significant numbers. This desert, a feature of Africa that has existed for about seven million years off and on, acts as a kind of geographic fence keeping species regionally landlocked. As the climate moderates, there exists the opportunity for species to move through holes in the geographic fence. Prior to this period,

H. sapiens, unlike *H. erectus* and others, had been mostly confined to the lower half of Africa. Of course, you should not visualize a mass exodus occurring one spring afternoon seventy thousand years ago. This most successful period of migration likely continued over several hundred if not thousands of years off and on.

You should be aware that this entire progression-of-our-species hypothesis is highly speculative and is based almost exclusively on DNA analysis. The truth is we don't exactly know much about our origin. Regardless, science informs us that once having a substantial presence outside the homeland of Africa, *H. sapiens* eventually interbred with previously established subpopulations. The latest DNA analysis indicates our species crossbred with other hominin species such as *Homo neanderthalensis* (a.k.a. Neanderthal). This crossbreeding between species of hominins and interbreeding of subpopulations of *H. sapiens* helps to explain why our species exhibits so many variations to this day. The skin tones and other superficial physical differences, which had evolved separately within specific geographic regions, were then reintroduced into the larger gene pool of the more recent African *H. sapiens*. A great deal of debate still exists about the specifics represented above. Nonetheless, DNA and other related data support this, our "out of Africa" story.

It is worth noting that hominins, the more human subset of the great apes of which our species is one variety, would likely have preferred milder climates near water or dense cover. One may be tempted to wonder what physical evidence we have lost due to changes in weather, terrain, and sea level over hundreds of thousands of years. Ultra-thinking leads me to consider that a huge amount of evidence is buried within the sands of the Sahara itself. With the Sahara being subject to a period of temperance, one would assume significant populations simply chose to migrate through the Sahara region directly whenever possible, rather than around this desert. Could there be *H. sapiens* evidence buried under the vast dunes of the Sahara? Some of the latest research on the Saharan region points to evidence that documents that as recently as eight thousand years ago the Sahara was a vibrant ecosystem complete with rivers and lakes. If we truly wanted to find our oldest civilizations, we should be digging the sands of extinct Saharan rivers instead of simply searching every cave on the planet.

The dinosaurs, existing millions of years before our species but for a much more extended period, left abundant fossil records. By comparison, one would be shocked at how little physical evidence we have in support of our accepted theories regarding *H. sapiens*. Our best evidence includes one 286 thousand-year-old partial skull, one 210 thousand-year-old partial skull, and two 190 thousand-year-old partial skulls. At about one hundred thousand years, things improve a bit. We have a few more skulls and miscellaneous bones up through about fifty thousand years ago; only then does direct evidence become more plentiful. Unfortunately for anthropologists, groups probably numbered no more than ten to forty individuals, their bones were relatively frail, and due to the adaptability of our ancestors, their range was broad.

Another important point that is not commonly known needs to be addressed. Our species is certainly not the most successful species of great ape, in terms of durability, to walk this planet over the past several million years. In fact, there are indications through DNA analysis that at one point within the last seventy thousand years (possibly coinciding with the Toba volcanic eruption) there may have been as few as one thousand breeding pairs of *H. sapiens* on the planet. When you consider hominids, and specifically great apes, you can confirm for yourself the success of a truly robust survivor. The closest currently living cousin to man, the chimpanzee, has likely been on our planet at least twenty times longer than our species. While it is true that the intelligence of this animal could be compared to that of a two-year-old human, one would have to admit that if survivability is the measurement, the common chimp, an intelligent, tool-using species of ape, has been more successful than *H. sapiens*.

Neanderthals and *Homo floresiensis* (a.k.a. Flores man) also managed to roam our earth far longer than *H. sapiens*, and these are only two of what could be more than a dozen species of human-like apes. There have probably been tens of successful hominins species over the past few million years. It is entirely possible that some of these species maintained very isolated populations. Could they have mentally constructed a narrative in which, as part of their beliefs in the meta, they needed to burn their dead? Is it possible we find no evidence of the existence of advanced hominins because as a species they destroyed the record? Still, what little evidence we find confirms that hominins such as Flores man, Denisovan, and Neanderthal man coexisted for tens of thousands of years with our species. Did any other intelligent hominin, discovered or not, construct a motorcycle? No, not likely. But did they, could they, build an ice sculpture, communicate in a manner since forgotten, or use science that involved the natural energy field produced by living organisms hundreds of thousands of years before we ever evolved? That is something to ponder. Many of us have Ultrathoughts that accept the likelihood that soon science will document that *H. sapiens* doesn't deserve its commonly accepted rank as the most intelligent species of hominins to have ever graced this Earth.

Cave art and fossilized bones found near stone tools persuade archeologists to think that *H. sapiens* began to think in a more modern way fifty thousand years ago. However, we can't be sure whether the cave art or tools found were created by our own or another species within the hominin subfamily of hominids. It is not only possible but likely that Neanderthal was the originator of at least some of these achievements of art, and certainly the use of tools is not exclusively a trait of *H. sapiens*. Countless species use tools, including birds.

Some biologists are open to the idea that an extinct but highly intelligent species could have developed a society that we will never understand. Evidence such as the communicative ability of whales or the intelligence of certain species of Coleoidea (squid, cuttlefish, and octopi) offers a mere glimpse of the barely understood capabilities of life. Octopi have societies, as do whales, ants, and birds.

These social orders are so alien to our human sensibilities that understanding their purpose and complexity presents a challenge. For instance, we view an ant as a simple animal. But the individual insect is not what we should focus on, rather the ant organism whose intelligence resides through the collective group that builds, hunts, and successfully competes with other organisms in its environment. The ant colony is the organism of life. Looked upon in this way, ants have been more successful than *H. sapiens*. The ant organism has been on the planet for 140 million years; *H. sapiens* less than one-fifth of one percent that long.

Directing our discussion back to modern humans, when evaluating fossils some scientists are quite confident that we are not even the most intelligent hominin amongst those very few species of which we are aware. They base their conclusions on brain size calculations using the fossils of other extinct hominin species less than fifty thousand years old. At that time, more intelligent species of human-like apes may have lived on the planet.

In conclusion, I would like to mention an intriguing research project that was reported in 2017. Well-respected Japanese scientists documented finding stone tools within a soil sediment layer in China dated at 2.1 million years ago. Recalling that our species is no more than three hundred thousand years old, assuming the scientists are correct in their dating these tool builders lived nearly two million years before *H. sapiens*!

- How far could they have evolved socially or scientifically before they became extinct?
- Did these users of stone, 2.1 million years ago, survive to evolve for one hundred thousand or one million years beyond that date?
- What further evidence will be discovered regarding their specific existence?
- If their population remained extremely small, will we ever find any additional evidence?
- Could their population have been limited to such a small area that a simple virus wiped them out although they may have developed a sophisticated society and even advanced medical techniques?
- We must admit it is also entirely possible that either the dating is wrong or there are other circumstances (maybe the tools themselves were simply buried) that would discredit this entire story.

We may never understand the answers to these questions. Regardless of their level of intelligence, scientific advancement, or long-term success, our ancient cousins in China have passed, and we are the only surviving human-like ape species. There are several theories as to why this is the case. However, it should not be blindly assumed that our survival occurred because we had superior intelligence to our genealogical brethren.

CHAPTER 10

HOW SMART WAS SHE?

We are smarter than ever. That is a bold but true statement, and it is accepted by the majority of people. While the words *smarter* and *true* demand some clarification, speaking colloquially, the statement stands.

Would a young woman living three thousand, thirty thousand, or one hundred thousand years ago think herself smarter than her ancestors? While your first response to this question may be yes, I contend that no, she would not automatically view herself as brighter than anyone from the past. She may believe she was clever enough, but instinctively she would understand that she was still naïve about many important issues. She may have seriously contemplated some of these issues while others were just not relevant to her daily existence.

Although the topic is the subject of much debate depending upon how one defines the word *intelligence*, most anthropologists agree that the intelligence of our species has not significantly improved since our origin some 250 thousand years ago. With that said, it is true that as a species our overall intelligence test *scores* continue to increase as time passes. There are a variety of reasons for this that are beyond our discussion. Regardless, don't confuse an IQ score (intelligence quotient measurement) with basic intelligence. The young woman living in a cave or bison skin tent some one thousand lifetimes before our own was every bit as intelligent as we are. We have more knowledge at our disposal, but we do not possess more innate intelligence than our predecessors.

It is theorized that if that young woman had a child, that child raised by you today would be indistinguishable from classmates.

Smartness, on the other hand, is a product of self-perception, ego, and the perceptions of others. One considered smart isn't automatically deemed intelligent. In common speak today, we even consider a phone smart, provided it has access to a database of knowledge. Of course, in the absence of the autonomous ability to apply said knowledge, a phone wouldn't be considered intelligent.

Intelligence is the capacity to know, interpret, and apply skill in the acquisition of more knowledge. The statement implies the ability to act with intent. Knowledge is the mind's accumulation and application of wisdom learned or otherwise known instinctively. Our species has the same potential to interpret and apply skills as it had thousands of years ago. An infant born tens of thousands of years ago, if immersed in our society today, would fare as well as you or I. Whether one uses an app-based map service or had used broken twigs to mark a trail home a hundred thousand years ago is irrelevant; our raw intelligence has basically been constant for many millennia. Unlike an orangutan or chimpanzee, our ancient relatives could think spatially and use abstract thought. An ordinary *H. sapiens* who was a hunter-gatherer roaming the plains of Africa could ponder how person D would react if person C thought person B was going to do something to person A. The woman of the past could comprehend the impact of seasonal weather patterns and what foods were beneficial to her body, and she cooperated with her friends just like you and I.

How would she have handled an intellectual challenge? She undoubtedly used trial and error after first thinking about her options. Upon repeated failure, she would have used logic or even experimental methods in analysis of the challenge. She would have "asked" around. The quotation marks are intentional because we have no definite idea as to when the first language evolved. Although speaking may have been accomplished by many hominin species as early as 1.75 million years ago, according to several scholars, rules of more complex language were probably developed within the last fifty thousand to one hundred thousand years as generations of humans began to hone their language skills. Development of these skills of complex language and the ability to pass them down to successive generations facilitated a more effective exchange of knowledge. This period is often called "The Human Revolution," the point in which we became behaviorally modern. Because complex language facilitates a more effective use of information, language may be the key component in the success of our species, not intelligence. Were complex language and its resulting behaviors truly unique to our hominin species? We may never know, but it is certainly probable that other species of hominins used some type of actual language as a means of augmenting simple grunts or whistles.

Regardless of how our ancestors chose to communicate frustration or inquiry, if an answer to a question couldn't be found, our person of the past would either conceptualize the mystery as unsolvable within her mind or set the problem aside as something to be addressed later. Unlike *H. sapiens* of the 21st century, it is doubtful she chastised herself as being dumb for not knowing the answer. Without internalizing a concept that labeled her as being dumb, she would not have believed herself to be smart. She probably approached most issues rationally, accepting the conclusion that the problem was either solvable or not. That answer came from her own mind or acceptance of the opinion of her group, and until that knowledge or belief was proven wrong, she had her truth—just like you and me.

Occasionally a significant puzzle would arise having no identifiable solution. For example, local game or fish simply fail to arrive as had previously been the pattern. Having a vivid imagination, the young woman may have considered the answer to lie in an otherworldly or abstract state. For some problems, she might have placed her faith in the wisdom of a shaman or group leader. Even though physically present, the shaman would not represent either the physical realm of science or the spiritual realm of the Godhead; reality for her was a blend of both. To refer to the wisdom of another would establish her acceptance as fact that she did not personally understand and chose to rely on the opinion of another. If the opinion was respected, she incorporated the view into her reality.

Today, many and probably most of us construct a personal narrative that leans heavily toward a physical reality. We don't necessarily think differently than she did, but our orientation is certainly different. When faced with an unsolvable problem, we typically assume that at some point science, a philosophy of thought based on the scientific method, will provide an answer. We certainly rely on the opinion of others, but we tend to assume that outside opinion is bolstered by objective evidence that our advisor either has or understands better than we do.

Even individuals who profess belief in a spiritual religion would not typically place their faith in the spiritual realm at first pass. Should one see a curious event, say the sudden fall of a bird from the sky, we would not immediately accept an unknown meaning. We would assume science knows why this occurred. Such an occurrence was no unexplainable miracle of the spiritual. Therefore, we would seek a logical or scientific solution to the question of the falling bird. To do otherwise would seem pointless. This wasn't always the automatic response. This modern behavior represents a shift in humanity; we tend to trust only in that which we believe can be known through science.

Individuals today elect to overrule their natural willingness to accept a spiritual truth by conditioning the mind to deny any meta possibility. This isn't particularly hard to do when an individual is immersed in a secular society. Unfortunately, once lost, the ability to appreciate the spiritual frequently proves difficult to relearn. However, with intent, spiritual awareness can be reactivated in most. I suggest that as a species, spiritual awareness is an innate capability.

My ultra-thinking leads me to believe that we continually evolve. In short, I believe that once our line loses innate spiritual awareness, we become a different type of human-like ape. An intelligent hominin for sure, but a species that will act and think differently. A more thorough exploration of my ideas on this particular subject is presented in book three, *Forbidden Philosophy*.

CHAPTER 11

BELIEF THEN AND NOW

In use of the term "reality," people today tend to automatically conceptualize only the physical realm. Without doubt the mind-myth constructed by postmodern persons living in a mechanized society seems to validate only that which they can touch, see, smell, taste, or feel. This is a very recent phenomenon, and humanity hasn't always segregated concepts of physical from spiritual within the mind. Historically, we didn't find it necessary within our minds to deny any possibility of an unknown. In fact, mankind seemed to encourage faith in the notions of the metaphysical realm. Societal belief and religion were both catalysts and products of man's attempts to implore the mind to build a value system inclusive of an unknowable Godhead force. This spiritual realm of the Godhead served as the catchall explanation for much of life's mysteries. Unexplainable or illogical events were simply attributed to the Godhead force. Over time, as philosophies came into vogue, specific societies further integrated unsupportable beliefs into their daily lives. As seen in the beliefs of ancient Egypt, India, and societies of the Mediterranean basin, human existence has included some level of spiritual consideration for tens of thousands of years.

Some anthropologists believe the dawn of those first thoughts of the Godhead began in unison with the development of complex language skills fifty thousand years ago. Others claim *H. sapiens,* and possibly other extremely primitive hominin species, in general, did so far earlier. The logic behind such a belief deals with the idea that since great apes of today seem to have some limited capacity to imagine, certainly any far more advanced hominins could intellectualize the metaphysical realm of the Godhead regardless of any parallel development of language. Furthermore, although there is no evidence, some are open to the idea that many intelligent animals, living or extinct, possess the innate ability to conceptualize the spiritual. The jury is split. We can't say whether our species is innately predisposed to accept the spiritual and seek the Godhead or whether this apparent characteristic of humanity came about as a byproduct of the acquisition of complex language skills.

Regardless, concepts of the spiritual have evolved over millennia, but one might wonder if we are beginning to buck the trend line. In the past couple hundred years it has been noted that, regarding philosophical concepts of the spiritual, our species appears to be doing one of two things: we are naturally evolving away from acceptance of metaphysical concepts, or we are making a conscious decision to suppress our innate spiritual inclinations. This trend may not be obvious to a person who has either experienced some newfound sense of enlightenment or whose circle of peers are enthusiastic advocates of the spiritual. Still, the percentage of individuals who profess a serious belief in spiritual religion is rapidly falling.

As a person puts their faith in the religion of science, they come to view believers in the unproven spiritual religions as primitive and less educated. As a result, within the mind-myth of some, spiritual thoughts are forbidden. This overt exclusion will either suspend any further evolution of meta concepts within the mind or affect the biology of the species over time. Either way, a denial of the spiritual by humanity will alter our perception of reality. The pace of this change continues to escalate as humanity obtains more knowledge—particularly scientifically supported knowledge. The religion of science may soon frame most interpretations of reality.

The acquisition of knowledge is not inherently a bad thing, but curiously, many ancient or sacred texts seem to warn that the obtainment of knowledge could lead to challenges for humanity. Are we today experiencing these challenges in full force? Indeed, if the spiritual realm itself does not exist, the entire issue is moot, and science or any knowledge derived would deserve our complete trust. But this book takes a position in support of an actual spiritual realm and values the Ultrathoughts of the ancients. I give credence to the wisdom of old, and therefore I have done some serious ultra-thinking on several questions.

- What was the purpose of many stories told by the ancients, warning us of knowledge as if it somehow were evil?
- Did shamans, prophets, or tribal leaders merely write to keep the "ignorant masses" at bay, having their own selfish reasons for doing so?
- Were ancient texts merely fables passed down for entertainment?
- Were stories or fables promoted as some sort of man-made yet benevolent wisdom?
- Is it possible the sacred teachings themselves had been transmitted directly from a spiritual realm of the Godhead spiritual force?
- Did the authors of ancient texts glean some sort of unique or keen understanding from a source not yet understood?

- Do certain long-held religious beliefs have a purpose for the betterment of humanity when actively infused into the physical reality we experience?

Regardless of the unanswered questions above, over the past few hundred years the magnitude of available knowledge of our physical reality has exploded. Many religious traditions and beliefs have been decimated during the same time frame, concurrent with the growth of a secular non-spiritually oriented society. These statements are not in dispute. I surmise established myths, religions, and societal beliefs that go beyond the physical are in decline, but not because we have evolved. Spiritual awareness is suffering as a direct result of the rise in acceptance of scientific dogma. The unintentional worship of the religion of science is capturing the mind of the person who simply has not nurtured his or her innate spiritual tendencies. The spread of this movement, secular materialism, is simply overwhelming the individual's casual attempt to maintain spiritual awareness. It has often been said that reason kills faith. I would qualify the statement. If reason kills faith, it is secular materialism that buries the corpse.

The delineation line of the physical realm is expanding aggressively into the spiritual realm as never before, and far fewer individuals are willing to openly accept the idea of a spiritual realm since such beliefs may appear baseless or foolish when compared to beliefs bolstered by science. This process is amplified in our connected world when we compare our personal beliefs to those of other societies. Let's reflect on why individuals often find it necessary to check or verify their faith in the spiritual. If faith is merely a belief and can't be proven, why would a person bother to verify their belief against others or any objective measure?

A quest to verify a simple faith through objective evidence points out a widespread misunderstanding regarding the concept of a meta faith or belief. Typically, a faith that originates not from blind acceptance of dogma but as a product of reason first starts as a somewhat skeptical belief. Then, as the mind comes to refine and internally justify the concept, a casual belief begins to gain the status of faith. Whether the faith originates first from reason or baseless indoctrination, some semblance of logic will typically justify even a meta faith. The mind of modern people seek reason, and reason is based on logic. As one further internalizes the faith, mind-myth construction builds a story in support of the faith, bolstered by reason twisted in a manner consistent with the faith that had seeded the mind. The narrative ages with the person. As various personal beliefs begin to sync with our personal faith, we each come to present our particular dogma to the world. Moving forward, without paying particular attention we see what we want to see and tend to disregard competing views. A believer builds a reality supported by a customized version of reason in support of a meta belief.

Of course, whether casual belief, truth, faith, or objective fact, each are still in actuality a matter of individual opinion. No seemingly objective truth exists forever, but back to the question. Why should one feel the need to check his or her belief?

The answer is likely not one but a combination of reasons. Certainly, a primary motive is that people wish to be emotionally connected to other members of the group. This is why peer pressure is so effective. The mind is constantly building and refining its internal story. Mind and ego seek validation of the belief held. The believer looks to their inner circle and the MOS for validation. If none is found, the seeker is at a crossroads. The search for answers either continues or is abandoned.

To question a belief is not only common, but a sign of a healthy active mind, not of a weak mind. A weak mind does not question; it's likely either dull or brainwashed. To question is the ultimate sign of intelligence. Bright people ask questions and tend to move through cycles of enthusiasm and doubt.

Lacking any objective proof from which to support belief, spiritual beliefs are ripe for constant questions. As an intelligent creature, you seek confirmation of your belief against actual evidence. Though most don't understand that a person will not find any actual confirmation of the meta anywhere but within the mind, doubting people strive for reassurance offered by objective evidence in support of their faith. This is the unfortunate state of a society that fails to understand the difference between an objective and a meta fact.

I suspect "seekers" of spiritual enlightenment come in two types. A seeker of objective proof, a left-brainer like myself, tends to seek enlightenment because they constantly attempt to make logical sense of their world. Comfort is provided when seemingly rational belief is supported by seemingly rational evidence. The second type, a seeker of emotional comfort, is more prototypical of a right-brainer who is inclined toward a quest for happiness. Given my premise that values meta concepts, naturally I characterize type two as being more of an actual seeker of true enlightenment. The right hemisphere of the brain is more oriented toward the meta; therefore, this type of thinker is more likely to obtain personal peace with regards to the Godhead. Type one seeks reason. Type two seeks enlightenment. I am innately type one but having created Ultrathoughts, despite my orientation, I can function as a type two seeker of true enlightenment.

In our individual mind, just as reason kills faith, doubt ultimately builds truth. As bizarre as that may sound, the statement is accurate. Doubt urges one to seek better answers: Ultrathoughts. Invariably, our important spiritual leaders—Confucius, Abraham, Jesus, Muhammed, Gautama Buddha, and Gandhi—experienced periods of questioning. Any seeker should take pride in that he or she is in the company of saints.

Engagement of your mind strengthens the brain and solidifies your unique story. When done in a whole-brain manner these contemplative thoughts lead to a more enlightened version of the person. The stronger the story, the stronger the faith that just may one day rise to a status of truth in one's own mind. Doubt brings forth confidence in a truth casually accepted. Faith and truth within the story of the mind create the reality of the individual.

I ultra-think that only one's willingness to doubt, an honest acceptance of one's own failure to know for sure, will build a strong faith. I suggest a strong faith is difficult for a thinking person to hold without first having doubt. A reflexive faith is fine enough for the naïve, but I am skeptical of its resilience in a world dominated by knowledge. Therefore, I suggest that everyone rethink their faith with an ultra-thinking mind. Indifference, not caring enough to consider what is true to you or to even challenge your own faith, is to deny your humanity and risk your historical faith. Neglect or continued apathy of the mind will likely destroy most any faith in the spiritual.

When any member of society bothers to compare his or her individual spiritual myth to another, the tendency is to view it as silly, malicious, or uninformed. Humans are fundamentally skeptical; they distrust the unfamiliar and tend to assume something negative. Spiritual beliefs are somewhat unique in that they seem to promote the idea that the observed knows something that may be truly important to the observer. That something becomes a subject of desire in the mind of the observer.

Contemplating a foreign belief takes work, while mocking the belief system of another is easy and reflexive. The goal of the ego is not understanding but protection of self. The mind has created a story and now owns its myth and associated beliefs.

Alternative views are always comprehended in comparison to our own internalized story. Observation of another who is engaged and quite happy in their adherence to a different faith can be quite offensive to the ego of the observer. If you are a spiritually oriented person, it is likely your spiritual beliefs are deeply seated within your narrative. A gleeful presentation of a foreign faith by another is an unintentional insult to your faith. The mind becomes defensive as it considers the real possibility that the foreign belief is truly more correct than one's own. The observer has two choices, degrade the new or contemplate the new. Degradation is easy, contemplation takes work.

When considering the beliefs of another, most religions have specific traditions that instruct believers on how to handle the nonbeliever. Often one religious member may be quite compelled by dogma to attempt conversion of the unenlightened, the assumption being that an intervention is necessary to set the nonbeliever straight for his or her own benefit. The most obvious example is Christian evangelism that seeks to spread the good news of the gospel, but basically every religion attempts to evangelize in some manner or another. Frankly evangelism is better than the second most common alternative: kill the infidel.

One group's tolerance toward another is not the rule. Humans are pack animals, not much different than wolves. Fundamentally, we are highly group-oriented. Groups compete, and as they do conflicts arise resulting in drama, stress, and often war. From such pressure, even a successful religious dogma tends to eventually weaken. Over time, as a dogma grows weary of constant challenges it tends to fall back on its last line of defense: a defense of tradition. Defense of tradition may be a noble idea, but such a strategy is flawed at multiple levels.

First, a reliance on tradition in defense of a belief denies the believer the ability to question his or her faith. As I stated previously, to doubt a faith will strengthen it in the end as the mind builds a mental construct in support of said faith.

Next, an absolute unwavering defense of tradition puts any associated religion in a lockdown mode. This prevents any further evolution of the faith within the broader society. A faith must maintain a degree of flexibility to stand the test of time. When not flexible, the religion and dogma become bound to outdated societal beliefs. Recall that reality and truth move within what I called a kind of carnival balloon of reality being segregated into a physical and spiritual realm. If the spiritual religion can't adapt as ideas of science evolve, a spiritual religion can't adequately defend itself. Traditions become dated, start to look silly even to the believers, and may ultimately be deemed fantasy in the mind. Once deemed fantasy, the mind will come to contemplate the religion as simply a historical tradition without purpose. Be aware that the philosophy of the religion is what's truly important, not the dogma. As a stalwart defensive continues over time, the Godhead philosophy is lost as a result of attempts to save the religion.

Societal beliefs and norms, not any particular spiritual dogma, set the standards for mankind. This dynamic eventually weakens all spiritual religions, but the process is exacerbated when a religion fails to evolve. The last surviving spiritual religion will eventually look stale and out of date in the view of the MOS. The religion of science is inherently adaptive, actively seeking a conquest of the unknown. When compared to stale spiritual tradition, science immediately takes the high ground of credibility in a mind that values objective proof. Only a non-spiritual religion will survive in an integrated and rapidly changing world; the religion of science wins in the end.

The religion of science has several key advantages over any spiritually based dogma. Fundamental to science itself is the creation of a hypothesis (the creation of a supposition). The scientific hypothesis is then subject to consideration through objective measurement. Objective proof, when measurable, is deemed reliable in support of a hypothesis or disproving of the hypothesis. Either way, objectivity is simply a measurement to gauge a hypothesis, also known as a theory, conjecture, or belief. Unlike spiritual beliefs, scientific beliefs are in the unique position of having a commonly accepted basis (mathematics) from which one can make evaluations that have come to be shared among societal members. Members of the society can unite in agreement by accepting objective measurement as validation of a truth or not.

Another advantage scientific belief has over spiritual belief is that a modern secular society promotes the physical realm. This is often the result of societal values that elevate materiality and consumerism in our daily lives. An ample supply of everything from food to electricity to fossil fuel is deemed the simple result of science. Furthermore, the very structure of modern society itself is based on scientific models. Modern society functions because of scientific laws, whether they are expressed as economic, environmental, social, criminal, or civil laws. Societies based on scientifically supported materialism can't help but suppress belief in the spiritual as they become successful.

An additional and potentially insurmountable advantage exists for science. We have become fundamentally attracted to the stuff of a modern mechanized society. A modern mechanized world is a planet oriented toward the physical pleasures of existence. Unlike a spiritual, religious dogma that promotes ideas of some future benefit in the afterlife, a mechanized society and the science that facilitated it promise ample rewards in the here and now, not after death. Realistically, the trappings of materialism have much more appeal for the living person happily indulging in physical pleasures than the vague promise of ill-understood spiritual rewards in the unknown future.

This way of life for the commoner is a new chapter for humanity. Human existence millennia ago was not engulfed in material pleasures. Life was a struggle for all but a very select few. Kings, nobles, and a few wealthy merchant elites certainly had access to material rewards, but most of the population could not realistically expect such a lifestyle. One who is struggling with an empty belly is not obsessed with getting a new smartphone. Years ago, the population was not so spiritually blinded in pursuit of material goods. The material focus of individuals within modern secular society is a principal cause of people losing their spiritual focus. This facet of our modern culture has and will continue to accelerate. Technology rapidly spreads the myth of an ideal mechanized existence, a reality of the mind-myth that promises endless physical pleasures.

As the trend continues, this lack of focus may lead to a complete lack of spiritual awareness. It is entirely possible we are already observing these effects today. If this trend continues in the coming decades, we may find that most if not all of humanity will have lost an innate spiritual awareness. There would be no need to suppress a meta yearning; people will have evolved to lose the inclination. *H. sapiens* might evolve to a state where the species no longer possesses a genetic predisposition to imagine the spiritual.

This change would be a stunning transformation for humanity—a further evolution of our species. The degradation of all spiritual belief leading to a variation in the genes of *H. sapiens* may seem very unlikely. However, although biology is unclear as to how genetic modification occurs, some of our most advanced research in genetics and epigenetics appears to lend credence to the idea that learned behaviors are literally passed on through our genes. Certainly, genes don't operate in isolation and are influenced by countless factors, but it is very likely attitude and opinion can be passed on from parent to offspring through DNA. Not so long ago most human beings, even the giants of science, respected ideas in support of the unknown spiritual realm, and even if they could not adequately explain why or how, they accepted that they could not know all.

Although religious dogma and enthusiasm for spiritual belief vary wildly between cultures, societies generally have maintained some trace of meta belief. Such beliefs have historically been considered worthy, despite the fact that they could not be proven. Those attitudes are on the decline across the globe. The reason may have at least something to do with cultural influence impacting our genes over the last few hundred years. Various anti-spiritual dynamics may be starting to manifest their impact on our species.

While certainly not all, many academics today besmirch the existence of the spiritual in their support of scientific dogma. These people may not be outright naturalists, but certainly they pooh-pooh the idea of the Godhead. Some may simply assume that they believe what they say for whatever reason, but the apparent loss of spiritual awareness by many, whether academic scholars or not, brings up some interesting questions.

- Why would so many intelligent individuals today hold such distaste for the spiritual realm, in direct opposition to the intellectuals of past millennia?

- Is our science so absolute that acceptance of any unanswerable question is naïve?

- Hasn't it always been accepted that the most intelligent people are those who are able to admit they don't know it all? Smart people ask questions and don't blindly follow the crowd.

- Is it possible we are already seeing DNA variations or epigenetic influences in flux that are impacting what had been an innate longing for spiritual comfort within our species?

- Is the loss of spiritual awareness the forfeiture of what makes *H. sapiens* different from any other living organism on earth?

As you ultra-think these questions in the coming days let me leave you with a story whose theme is quite common across the globe.

You're probably familiar with the story of Adam and Eve in the Garden of Eden, as told in Genesis of the ancient Hebrew Bible. The first section, the "creation narrative," gets most of the attention, but as the story continues its most important message is revealed in allegory.

God warns each person not to partake of the tree of knowledge, with the fruit of knowledge represented by an apple. This warning strikes many as odd. Why wouldn't God want them to know as much as they could? The story rings as being fundamentally anti-knowledge or even anti-progress. Some consider this to be the author's attempt to protect accepted spiritual dogma by instructing followers to stay unsophisticated in their thought. To do so would help preserve the status quo, thereby reserving refined and informed knowledge for a select few.

At first read, it does appear that the text implies one should not question authority and simply follow the teachings of God's chosen messengers. But I suggest a more in-depth interpretation of this story. This was possibly a message of compassion toward humanity—an attempt to save us and keep the person spiritually aware.

The story may be warning Adam and Eve, who are enjoying carefree living in paradise, that knowledge itself will negatively alter their lives, their reality—not that knowledge is evil but that its pursuit would compromise paradise. We can't necessarily comprehend paradise, but we can understand the use of allegory.

The story uses the apple as a metaphor for knowledge, and Eve couldn't understand why biting such a wholesome apple would be wrong. She was asked to have faith in the message and set aside her desire. The warning was to be taken seriously despite its illogical nature. She needed to have faith in God. Though it made no sense, partaking in knowledge somehow risked their relationship with God. Reason would kill faith and destroy paradise. Being tempted by desire and eventually losing her fear, she took the forbidden bite. She chose knowledge over ignorance, sacrificing paradise in the end.

Are we making these same risky choices every day, losing our faith in meta truth in favor of a quest for objective knowledge? Are we truly better off as a result? In a material sense the answer is clearly: yes. Still, overall, is it truly worth losing any hope of living in paradise for eternity?

PART IV

CHAPTER 12

DYNAMIC TRUTH

The brain shares specific characteristics with physical muscles. No one disputes that if a muscle is not exercised it will waste. As we age it becomes obvious. The biology is different of course, but the brain suffers a similar fate. It has been proven that the brain loses certain abilities, like the ability to effectively navigate directions, unless it is regularly challenged to do so. Research involving the use of smartphones is building a case that our technology is making people dumb. Technological advancement often leads to mental laziness. A strong mind is an exercised mind, a fact accepted universally among psychiatrists and gerontologists. Your sense of direction and ability to concentrate are among hundreds of capabilities that require exercise to stay sharp. For example, a newborn infant can interpret complex and nuanced facial expressions but would lose the ability if deprived of the opportunity to use it. Innate social skills, which are enhanced through subconscious interpretation of the facial expressions of another, are lost without practice. Patterns are created within the brain by a network of neurons that becomes more physically robust through repeated use. Like a path through a field of tall grass, if the pattern of neurons is not used, it is overwhelmed by a myriad of other patterns overlaying its original trail.

Be reminded that very little of the brain is hardwired, so to speak. Left or right-brain orientation and the inclination of particular regions of the brain to perform particular tasks don't restrict the capabilities of the brain. The brain is incredibly complex and flexible. Research on memory shows how flexible the brain can be.

For years scientists have believed that memories, unlike functional tasks, are not generally relegated to particular brain regions or hemispheres. Memories were thought to actually physically exist as firing patterns of cells making up neuron networks. These networks exist in countless locations within our brain. Though these firing patterns of cells can string for inches if not several feet in length, it has been assumed that if we could find the location of a certain repeated memory pattern, we could literally cut it out of the brain. However, in recent years this hypothesis has come under increased scrutiny. Some researchers are inclined to believe that memories may not be stored anywhere in the brain at all. There are indications that memories are somehow regenerated on the go, as needed. There may be a routine location in reflection of a memory, but not a fixed pattern or location. This type of research may soon undo decades of scientific theory regarding brain specifics, but frankly, much of this is pure conjecture. Science has little more than clues as to how the brain actually works.

With regards to the individual mind, the explanations offered by neurologists are even more vapid. They don't even know if the mind is a product of the brain, let alone how the mind could be created by a collection of cells. Nevertheless, the task is accomplished; we do have a story as a component of our mind. Brain and mind interact in a manner that facilitates mind-myth, all while managing the affairs of the physical body.

No matter how old one is or how inflexible his or her base orientation toward enlightenment appears to be, new ideas and concepts can gain credibility within the individual's mind. Learning and exploiting one's capability of deep thoughts requires practice since while thinking is innate, ultra-thinking and the resulting Ultrathoughts are not. Not only do individuals lose the mental sharpness necessary to think deep thoughts; they lose their ability to focus through the neglect of their brain. The brain can stupefy, especially as a person ages, if not given mental stimulation. But just as any person at any age can build muscle, the vigor of the brain can be renewed with patience and practice.

Unfortunately, science today is documenting that the brain function of even very young individuals can degenerate quickly from lack of interaction with stimuli. A society of stupefied beings, young and old, is not likely to think deep thoughts or maintain a sense of the spiritual. Indoctrination undeniably works to limit one's ability to think, as any parent, spiritual leader, or psychiatrist can attest. Human beings can be programmed not to think.

Interestingly, without any scientific proof to support his views, philosopher and political scientist Karl Marx spoke of such phenomena in the 1840s. Here I bring up Marx and contemplate governance in general, not to think about politics but for our minds' consideration of the spiritual realm. He suggested an entire political philosophy, collectively referred to as Marxism, where exploitation would be aided by the removal of the concept of God and religion from society. Marx knew people without God are more likely to seek solace in the comfort of the group or political leadership. They are programmed not to conceptualize anything abstract, be it God or spiritual happiness. A mentally dull person is a hollow, empty person who seeks solace outside the spiritual when all spiritual belief is denied either overtly by controlling leaders or inadvertently through atrophy of the brain. In Marxism, one's economic group of peers provides comfort, aided by the government, to the stressed individual. Every student of political science for the past hundred years has learned this dynamic. When stressed, people seek spiritual comfort if they have accepted within their mind that spirituality itself is worthy of consideration. When spiritual comfort is not available, material comfort will do, but if material and spiritual comfort are not available, the only thing left is the comfort of one's group and rulers.

This interplay of the mind is particularly interesting regarding thoughts of the Godhead within the context of today's society. While a spiritually vacant person today may or may not seek comfort through a political structure, what is common is a focus on the material. The best literal representation of this result is the recent growth in the number of self-described "shopaholics" and even hoarders. Not to say this applies to every shopaholic, but it's safe to assume that such a person has a spiritual void they are trying to fill through material stuff. People need comfort. In the past, belief in the spiritual was such a comfort. In times of stress, people went to their place of worship to pray and seek the spiritual. Remove spiritual awareness and respect for these beliefs, substitute the material pleasures, and you create individuals who overindulge to soothe themselves or fill a void in their life. The goal of a secular society is to remove the spiritual premise from consideration.

Be they Marxist, capitalist, or any other, the government seeks control of the group, and typically considers Godhead beliefs a threat to such control. The easiest manner to achieve the goal of removing God from society is to substitute a distractive culture immersed in materialism. Citizens voluntarily deny the spiritual in favor of their material pursuits. A socialist or communist government, being less focused on material pleasures, tends to rely more on the constant promotion of a "one for all" myth as a means to remove thoughts of God. Dictatorships, being authoritarian, are very likely to attempt a forceful exclusion of God concepts. Regardless of the method used, once an individual becomes aware that thoughts of God are forbidden, the mind tends to focus on the spiritual. For this reason, governments prefer a slow and steady removal of God from society rather than an overt ban of spiritual belief if at all possible.

Today, the Chinese system of government is the ultimate tool in the suppression of the spiritual. The communist Chinese system, while maintaining a strict political rule, has adopted an economic model like that of the United States. The system elevates the material, indirectly suppresses the spiritual, and being based on Marxist philosophy, the country also continually promotes the collective. This model, a blend of economic capitalism and Marxism, has been very successful by most accounts. If unequivocally proven a success, the Chinese system will likely become the norm throughout the world within the coming decades.

The only remaining religion after spiritual religious beliefs have been shunned will be the religion of science. Ultimately, this will have an impact on the individual. Just as you would lose your social skills without human interaction or your ability to conceptualize a roadmap through a continued reliance on GPS (Global Positioning Satellite technology), a person immersed within a secular society will lose what had been an innate spiritual sense. Mental capabilities must be exercised to be maintained. The MOS, being influenced by a collective of individuals, further devolves to suppress the spiritual; the entire process is somewhat circular. The more society devalues the spiritual, the more individuals do the same, and the cycle continues.

Maintenance of spiritual traditions that are active and fully engaged and/or ultra-thinking the meta may prove to be a person's only defense against this threat to spiritual awareness, mental atrophy. When an entire society becomes secular, it is completely left to the person to keep concepts of the spiritual alive in the mind. Today we still possess this ability. Therefore, even if we have lost or barely maintained any spiritual mindfulness, our biology assists us in our attempt to regain awareness. As a muscle can be strengthened, so can the mind, but regaining mindfulness requires serious effort once a mental task has been neglected. For how many generations will *H. sapiens* maintain the ability to conceptualize the spiritual, to "know" God, in the face of the coming modern global society?

That which makes *H. sapiens* unique among animals living today, and for all we know among any other hominin who ever lived, is our ability to conceptualize the spiritual. Most of us somehow manifest a spiritual yearning that urges us toward an understanding of our metaphysical purpose. Lose this ability, and we are merely common animals. Could we ever lose what makes us human? Some would say no; this capability is in our genes. Others would remind us that our DNA changes over time. Would our ego, our sense of superiority, ever allow us to become "common animals?" My Ultrathoughts lead me to believe the ego itself may be the problem.

CHAPTER 13

EGO, DEFENDER OF MYTH

Our ego is a mixed blessing. While there is no doubt that it has been helpful in our competition for domination of the planet it can, in some ways, limit our mental faculties.

The primary purpose of our ego is self-protection. Ego may have evolved as a direct result of our physical frailty, but it has proven critical to our individual success within a society of humans. The ego leverages protection by instilling self-confidence and bravado, each useful tools when facing a fierce saber-toothed cat or a simple band of literary critics. Another positive aspect of the ego is its ability to aid the mind in protection of its myth. We gain confidence in our truth as it matures under the protection of ego. Mature stories built on confidence are memorable. Recall is enhanced by ego, and thus the ego improves the function of the mind and contributes to the success of the species.

A well-known aspect of the ego is its tendency to generate pride. Pride inevitably suppresses or encourages one's willingness to take actions. Pride helps us appreciate risk that could lead to physical or mental harm. Ego-enhanced pride helps keep individuals in harmony with their peers, thereby improving the group's chance of success. Today we call this effect peer pressure, and working with the ego, it limits the individual's willingness to take a stand, a position, against the customs of the group. A person doesn't want to risk personal humiliation and ridicule by upsetting the norm.

The ego and the spiritual may clash. In the past, religious dogma, hand in hand with peer pressure, could keep individuals within the fold and support their bond with spiritual concepts. These days, societal pressure can dictate that thoughts of the spiritual are silly, unintelligent, or unsupportable. The dogma of science, the physical realm, may be considered by the collective as superior, and the individual would prefer not to question the accepted wisdom of the group. Whether one specific religion or a collection of religions of similar values, societies of the past generally promoted beliefs that acknowledged a superior unknowable realm. In modern society, given the collective secular norm, when the ego of the individual looks to the broader society it usually decides it is best to suppresses instinctive spiritual leanings.

CHAPTER 14

ULTRA-THINKING DEATH

Contemporary philosopher Bertrand Russell, author of "Philosophy for Laymen," explains the benefits of philosophical musings. He recognizes that definitive answers to his own questions won't be found, still he observes how important thoughts are to the person. Humans reflect like no other creature. Though he left no written word for our scrutiny, Socrates, two thousand four hundred years earlier, noticed the exact same nature in people. We need to think. It is a shame they're not around to educate us in person today.

We know of their ideas, and our culture is richer as a result. I sometimes wonder what worthy ideas have died with the unknown thinker. Maybe I shouldn't be so melancholy. It is possible that sometime soon our society will possess the technology necessary to catalog all ideas for posterity. You heard that right—all ideas of everyone. The essence of the person will then live on in the digital ether.

This is an offensive concept to some, but it is not particularly hard to believe. Even today, modern search engines are creating highly accurate algorithms that predict everything from your next purchase to your lifespan. Once modeled your ideas don't necessarily need to be recorded, simply calculated as needed. Of course, I should remind you that predictions will never be one hundred percent accurate, but they can be pretty darn close.

For a variety of reasons, certain folks like me contemplate the meta. So, I'll give you a wild thought to ponder. What if our *digital-self* is the eternal life we seek? It is evident that every person has tendencies and habits. These leave patterns in representation. Those patterns can be reduced to predictive mathematical formula. That is why algorithmic search technology is so efficient. The formula is using mathematics to predict your next move. These tendencies could be made timeless in digital form. Digital-you could live forever, eternally reaping the rewards and consequences of the model. The person you create today would then never die and remain a member of society. Could a composer still write and sell her songs as a digital version of herself? Is this the everlasting "life" spoken of in spiritual texts, condemned to whatever formula of life she creates today? If we live a hellish existence, are we choosing our fate for eternity? A full exploration of this idea would take another book, but the idea is worthy of ultra-thinking.

After restraining ideological predisposition in order to contemplate the outrageous, we can truly ultra-think any number of meta subjects—fun ones like the potential of our digital-self, or far heavier subjects. Given the importance of life, I believe a healthy mind should devote some time to the question of death. Only then can we ground our truth. Before moving further, given the extremely heavy nature of the topic, we must work hard to free the mind of presuppositions.

When asked to contemplate death, all of us will eventually consider questions like: What is the point or significance of *our* species of animal on this planet at this time? Why am I here? We do so because of our ego.

All of life's biggest questions revolve around us due to our immersive delusion. Frankly, if you seriously ultra-think that statement alone, the delusional reality to which I refer should be patently obvious. Regardless of the reason why, it is natural that a question of reality morphs into a question of self. René Descartes is credited with putting the matter succinctly: I think, therefore I am. He supposed that our very ability to ask the question infers our very existence and brought forth a series of Ultrathoughts centered around his belief.

I choose to accept his premise, building my foundational beliefs around an assumption that I exist as both a physical individual and a thinking person. The individual me is all that is my physical matter, while my person includes both the mind and essence of me in abstract presence.

Now let us reflect on what happens to the person when the individual passes away. For our purposes here, we will assume we have no opportunity to live on in digital form. That may one day change, but for now, once the person dies, the brain dies, and there is no chance that a formula can replicate the person.

When we reduce the issue to an extremely basic level, I suggest there are three primary options concerning the afterlife:

1. Naturalism: All I am is my biology. I am merely an individual; physical death ends my existence.

2. Monotheism or polytheism in any number of variations: I am more than my biological organism. I am both an individual and a person. That which is not my biology, the person, lives beyond my physical existence as a spirit, vapor, energy, or something else; call this a soul. Soul and God (or Godhead) may be related but are separate from each other.

    a. The newly freed soul reunites with or seeks to be near the Godhead.

    b. Reincarnation of the soul occurs when it returns to another body, be it human baby or another living organism, upon the passing of the prior life. In short, the human soul is recycled to inhabit another being.

3. Pantheism: The biology of the physical body has a soul-like component. I am both an individual and a person. However, this person—possibly ill-defined as a human soul—is merely a subset of the larger whole or universal Godhead. The physical death of an individual body is an inconsequential event in the broader context of the existence of the Godhead.

If one genuinely believes in option one, biology is all and death is the end, it seems that no further reflection is needed. A naturalist might promote this answer as scientific and rational. I suggest this answer is inherently incomplete without directly addressing several obvious logical flaws. For example:

- Why isn't our existence more like that of a pride of lions or tribe of chimps, where dominant individuals exploit any and every advantage?
- If we are common animals lacking any spiritual nature and the world operates under the model of Darwinism (survival of the fittest), why ever act morally toward those beyond your immediate group?
- Why would an individual enjoy any metaphysical experience, like a sunset or music?

These are a few out of a couple of dozen questions that flow in response to the "biology is all" answer. Furthermore, in my discussions with devout naturalists, or merely everyday well-educated adults, I run into an intriguing paradox of thought. Remember that a naturalist is one who states plainly, as fact, that the spiritual does not exist since the object, or God, can't be proven.

When queried as to how that proof is to be derived, the casual answer is that it is through science. As you've learned, scientific knowledge doesn't prove; it seeks to disprove a hypothesis. The point that the spiritual has not been proven does not validate or refute anything—a fact that anyone with even the most basic understanding of science should appreciate. My challenge to the naturalist is that while one may have the opinion or even an internalized truth of belief that biology is all there is, there will never be absolute proof of the conclusion. If the position can't be proven, why state that the reason for holding such a view is a lack of objective proof of the spiritual?

If an individual chooses to believe "biology is all," I simply ask one indulgence. Admit the position is technically a faith. This, like any faith, is incorporated into a philosophy of life, into one's delusional reality. Unlike the spiritually inclined, far too often the highly-educated post-modern naturalist doesn't consider themselves as having any faith or any belief in the meta at all.

Common logic is not on the side of the naturalist. Irrefutable physical proof that there is no God is a fantasy of the mind. All is an illusion within the mind. The naturalist is simply failing to cede the point.

What many naturalists seem to have forgotten is that most intelligent minds of the past openly contemplated the spiritual realm. They understood the difference between methodology and philosophy. Besides, they knew the simple expression of belief was no threat to science. I suggest many of these individuals logically deduced there was little chance of an afterlife or even Godhead presence. However, since they couldn't categorically deny the meta, they simply elected to believe for the simple reason that they lived a happier, more productive life as a result.

To internalize any answer in response to the question of life after death—be it the position of the naturalist, monotheist, polytheist, or pantheist—represents the creation of a personal faith or truth within your own delusional reality of mind. Your belief, once embedded, comes to frame further inclinations. A faith in the Godhead represents a toehold in the spiritual realm, a de facto denial of the "biology is all" supposition.

In the second book of the series, *Godhead Designs,* we'll explore Ultrathoughts of spiritual philosophy credited to several noted philosophers who are anything but naturalists. Before closing, let me leave you with an Ultrathought by noted global philanthropist and three-time world heavy weight boxing champion Muhammad Ali. He, like so many of us, bothered to ultra-think and had created an Ultrathought about the afterlife.

He was asked "What are you going to do when you retire from boxing?" After first joking with the youngster who posed the very serious question, Muhammad couldn't help but attempt to enlighten the child regarding a far more important subject, the afterlife.

> ***"[I'm going to] get myself ready to meet God, because God is watching me. He wants to know how did we treat each other? How did we help each other? So, this [existence] is a test to see where we spend our life. In Heaven, or Hell? And, that's Eternity! This is not your life! Your real self is inside you. Your body grows old, but your soul and your spirit never die. So, when I die if there's a Heaven I want to see it. God is testing us to see how we treat each other, how we live."***

This purposeful man lived an exhilarating life as he improved the lives of millions in Africa and elsewhere. He made a difference. To my knowledge, despite his bluster and chosen profession, he had no malice in his heart. Here's my question to you. Was his truth wrong?

CONCLUSION

In this first book of the series, we have explored some heavy concepts. Though we began with a carnival balloon in representation of a reality, we closed by taking on the heavy subject of death. Though I would never call you an Old Hippie or Old General, I did question the wisdom of simply continuing to accept your current ideology. I even challenged your personal perception of reality, truth, science, and God. Knowing my ideas are bit unusual, nevertheless, I pressed ahead to question all institutional dogma—particularly the non-spiritual religion of science. Though any belief is potentially worthy, I suggest a reevaluation of personal truth in hopes of creating a better whole-brain truth. Remember, yours is a choice, not a mandate from others.

I suggested nothing can be known beyond that which we think. As a result, you are a reflection of the self you have created. Finally, we discussed an ideal subject for ultra-thinking: death. In doing so we built a case for the premise that the question of life after death is logically meaningless from the view of a naturalist. On the other hand, for one who is spiritually aware, this same question is the ultimate topic, a perfect subject for an ideologically barren mind.

Keep in mind I have the utmost respect for you, and I appreciate you not being insulted by my premise. When I question your ideological leanings, I do so not because I think they are wrong, but because I know that a failure to question yourself limits your ability to be truly enlightened. If I didn't think I could help people live a more fulfilling life, I wouldn't have bothered to write in advocation of ultra-thinking. I wish nothing but a happy life for you.

My favorite parts of life are meeting thinking people and contemplating why we don't agree. This requires mutual respect. My fear is that our cooperative society is being undermined by self-immersion in our own ideological bubbles. This is exacerbated by our modern mechanized society, which allows us to consume media that reinforces our inclination.

You have completed this brief book, the very first of three. I know you are a thinker. Will you now attempt to be a poet, an ultra-thinker? Whether you are oriented toward thoughts of your logical-left or creative-right hemisphere, you want your truth. A poetic phrase is on your horizon, and soon after, a butterfly will emerge. You may even be a seeker of an ultimate truth, a Godhead truth. What better way to seek a quality truth of your mind than to create an Ultrathought?

Maybe you're not quite clear about the ultra-thinking premise or even have doubts about its worthiness. The second book in the series, *Godhead Designs*, will highlight the power of Ultrathoughts in hopes of urging you to ultra-think. The reader is introduced to some historical designs of the Godhead through a presentation in chronological order. I see an evolution of ideas and you may as well. In the interest of full disclosure, I start the presentation with a recap of own blueprint for the Godhead. By familiarizing yourself with my own design first, you will be better prepared to recognize any bias which remains in my descriptions of the Ultrathoughts of these master philosophers. The idea behind this exercise is to educate and help you build the confidence necessary to truly suppress your bias. In doing so, you'll urge your personal narrative toward fair consideration of fresh ideas. Historical ideology will be recognized, questioned, and ultimately suppressed. As you read you will grow to appreciate that the smartest minds of antiquity weren't so constrained by the MOS or their subconscious inclinations. You will start to do some ultra-thinking.

The mental giants of old simply took time to think; why don't you? I seek to persuade you to persist in ultra-thinking throughout your life. What better way to encourage you to do so than to show you that the greatest minds of old are no more special than you? I surmise that to think their incredible thoughts they practiced what I promote. Thinkers of old suppressed their ideology and thought from the whole brain. The book builds up to the Ultrathoughts Tripartite finale.

Forbidden Philosophy, book three, is where I lay my forbidden Ultrathoughts in front of the world and record them in the ether of the cosmos. It is a big step to take, and I have mixed emotions about presenting my ideas. What if I told you it is reasonable to believe, among other things, that extra-terrestrial aliens exist, time is not linear, reality is simply a product of "caring" enough to look for it, and quantum entanglement supports the premise that prayer works? Forbidden, or just plain stupid? You can decide in the somewhat random yet brief conclusion to the series.

As an ultra-thinker, you can accept my wild version of a truth while personally believing me to be absolutely wrong. We've found common ground simply by showing a willingness to listen to one another with respect and an open mind. I'll even buy you that venti Blonde Roast Veranda Blend. Me, I'll take some Kentucky Bourbon. You might understand why if you join me again.

"The Beginning is the most important part of the work."
Plato

CITATIONS

1. National Academy of Sciences (1984). Library Resource. https://ncse.com/library-resource/national-academy-sciences-1984

National Academy of Sciences (1999) "Science and Creationism." https://www.nap.edu/catalog/6024/science-and-creationism-a-view-from-the-national-academy-of

2. Rosen, Len. 2018. "Exceeding the Speed of Light Possible in a Quantum Experiment." *21st Century Tech*, March 13, 2018. https://www.21stcentech.com/exceeding-speed-light-quantum-experiment/

3. Saplakogu, Yasemin. 2019. "Faster-Than-Light Particles Emit Superbright Gamma Rays that Circle Pulsars." *Live Science*, April 29, 2019. https://www.livescience.com/65344-quantum-vacuum-gamma-rays.html

4. Buks, E., Schuster, R., Heiblum, M., Mahalu, D., and Umansky, V. 1998. "Dephasing in Electron Interference by a 'Which-Path' Detector." *Nature* 391, 871–874 (1998). https://www.nature.com/articles/36057.ris

5. Choi, Charles C. 2013. "Something from Nothing? A Vacuum Can Yield Flashes of Light." *Scientific American*, February 12,

2013. https://www.scientificamerican.com/article/something-from-nothing-vacuum-can-yield-flashes-of-light/

6. Hampson, Michelle. 2017. "Satellite Calls Earth on the Quantum Line." American Association for the Advancement of Science, June 14, 2017. https://www.aaas.org/news/satellite-calls-earth-quantum-line

GLOSSARY FOR FULL SERIES

collective mind (CM): Similar to *mind of society* as a societal attitude, belief, tone, style, and sensibility; a meta idea that does act with intent. Comparable to the idea of a *world soul* having a presence and/or relationship to the Godhead.

complex (dynamic) system: A system composed of many components that may interact with each other. Aggregate activity is nonlinear (not derivable from the summations of the activity of individual components), adaptive, and open. Variability is seen as an inherent property of the system although it typically exhibits a hierarchical self-organization under certain pressures.

dogma: A set of principles laid down by an authority and perpetuated by perception of dominance. A code of tenets or body of doctrine.

epigenetic: Relating to nongenetic influences on gene expression. A general term used to describe dynamics not fully understood by scientists in the field of genetics.

god/God: Superhuman presence, being, or force. Brahma, Zeus, Jesus the Christ, God of Abraham, and simply "God" are among various names used to describe a superhuman presence.

Godhead: A generalized or meta concept of God. The domain or realm of all that is godlike.

ideology: Your ideas wrapped around your personal mind-myth narrative.

indoctrination: The process of teaching someone ideas and standards with or without intent.

hard science: Often associated with the natural sciences; biology, chemistry, physics. Sciences associated with a well-defined methodological rigor.

Hellenist: A person speaking the Greek language whose outlook and way of life was significantly influenced by the Greek Empire of ancient times, regardless of heritage or geographic location.

Hellenistic era: Defined by Wikipedia.org as being from 323 BCE to 31 BCE, although dates assigned by other sources vary.

meta: Non-material, unknown, or spiritual.

metaphysical: See *meta*.

mind: Your ideas and concepts. Not quite so defined as to be a story, but similar.

mind-myth, narrative, personal story: The way you think. Your ideas woven into a metaphorical story that serves as a framework from which you perceive information.

mind of society (MOS): Societal attitude, shared beliefs, tone, style, and sensibility having no spiritual or physical presence other than the force of inertia. MOS is a meta idea that has no ability to act with intent.

monotheism: A belief in and associated worship of a specific and single God.

naturalism: see *religion of science.*

philosophy: Study and contemplation of the fundamental nature of knowledge, reality, and existence.

physical realm: The domain of reality dealing with the material substance of matter. Deals with the known or that which is deemed knowable.

polytheism: A belief in and associated worship of multiple gods.

quantum: Discrete quantity of energy. An expression used to describe a non-material presence of energy, momentum, or electric charge.

realm: Domain, area, kingdom.

religion: A belief in and associated worship of a theme, set of ideas, or controlling presence.

religion (spiritual): A belief in and associated worship of a superhuman presence.

religion (non-spiritual): Beliefs and worship that are not associated with any superhuman presence.

religion of science: A belief in and associated worship of a set of ideas that deny any superhuman presence. Naturalism or Darwinism.

science: A systematic methodology that organizes knowledge in the form of a testable hypothesis (informed guess).

scientific method: The methodology that involves observation, cognitive assumption, mathematics, and specific testing in an attempt to disprove a hypothesis.

soft science: Often associated with social sciences; economics, philosophy, sociology, psychology. Sciences ill-defined and less subject to a well-defined methodological rigor.

soul: A spiritual consideration that deals with the immaterial part of a being either human, other animal, and/or substance matter of life.

spiritual: The domain of belief, truth, or reality that deals with the immaterial, unknown, unknowable, and/or Godhead. All that is not within the physical realm.

ultra-thinking: An act of purposeful thinking in a manner that restrains personal ideology, indoctrinated belief, and existing expertise of the thinker as it forces the mind to actively seek outlandish new information.

Ultrathought: Deep contemplative thought, idea, or epiphany as a product of ultra-thinking.

world soul: A spiritual consideration that deals with the immaterial part of the cosmos, nature, universal consciousness, and self-awareness of a physical substance.

www.ingramcontent.com/pod-product-compliance
Lightning Source LLC
Chambersburg PA
CBHW021154020426
42331CB00003B/55
9781951731007